Table of Content

Chapter 1:

5 Scientific Tricks To Become Perfectly Happy

Being happy comes naturally. Almost everything around us makes us happy in a certain way. Being happy is a constant feeling inside a human being. They always tend to get satisfied, even at a minimum. Everywhere we look nowadays, we see things filled with this bright emotion. We tune to the songs written about happiness, we see posters at every corner about being happy, and most importantly, we have people who make us happy. Being happy comes freely, without any fee.

There are scientific ways to become happy because an average human is always looking for more.

Some ways in which you'll feel full at heart and eased at mind. A burst of good laughter is like medicine to the core. So, science has given us ways to take this medicine without and cautions. Being happy is one of the least harmful emotions. It binds people together. Even some forms have been scientifically proven to work in favor of our happiness. There is almost no end to those bright smiles on our lips or those crinkles by our eyes. As it said, smiling is contagious. And we all prefer to smile back at everyone who smiles at us automatically. Here are some scientific ways to be happy.

1. **Minutes Into Exercise**

It is proven that some exercise helps you to smile and laugh more. If there is an exercise to be happy with, then people would be sure to give it a try now and then. Exercise helps us to regulate our jaw muscle, so it will be easier to pass a smile next time. There is also meditation. It enables you to calm your mind and leads towards an easier life. It usually helps to keep you at peace so you'll feel happier towards the things that should make you happy. You'll start to get more content at certain or small items. It becomes a habit slowly to smile more, be more satisfied. Being happy also benefits others, and then they will be more inclined to be pleased towards you.

2. Get Enough Sleep

Another scientifically proven way to get happy is to sleep enough every night. It helps with the formation of a proper mindset towards your happiness in life. Sleeping at least 8 hours a day is a must for being happy; if not, the 7 hours would suffice enough for you to smile a little more. It keeps your mind and soul at a steady pace, which is inclined to keep us calm and collected. Keeping calm and organized is one of the factors to be happy. Wake up early to listen to the birds or go for a morning run. Keep yourself fresh in the morning to be a better and happier person. Early to bed is a wise men choice. So, get a sound slumber every night to have a sunny morning following you.

3. Take A Break Now and Then

Even the greatest minds need some rest, so it's only average for a human to get some rest after a long period of working day and night. Go on a vacation. Get a leave because life needs to be enjoyed through anything. Working all the time makes you dull and unhappy. So, make sure to take a break once in a while to start again with a fresh mind and perform a better duty. Don't load yourself with the things that won't matter in a few years. Take vacation so you'll have a more peaceful time ahead of you in your life.

4. Build Your Happy Place

People tend to get tired quickly and often by working all the time. All most of the time, vacation can't seem like an option. So, the best place to visit in such a situation is your happy place—a place you have created in your mind where you are so glad all the time. Just by imagining such a place, you get comfortable and tend to keep working and being pleased with the same time. Your happy place gives you joy, and you become a happier person overall. And it is just easier to carry your vacation with you all the time.

5. Count Your Achievements

A great way to be scientifically happy is to count all the achievements you have made so far. Even count little things like watering plants as an achievement because it gives you a sense of joy. Achievements tell you that you have done more in your life than you intended to, and you will get motivated to do more every time. It makes you believe in yourself and get you going only forwards. You get happy with the deeds you have done till now, and it helps you plan your next good achievement. You naturally become more inclined to fulfill your desires and needs. All the things you have done so far will make you feel beneficial to society and happier for yourself.

Conclusion

Being happy is a great feeling with a more remarkable result in life. So, smiling more won't do you any wrong; in fact, it may be good for you to stretch your jaw a little. Happiness doesn't discriminate, so it will be good to spread this scientific happiness as much as we can. Being happy gives us a sense of undeniable joy and a vision of a positive and bright future.

Chapter 2:

Happy People Are Optimistic

Beyond the simple reality that optimists are happier people (and happiness is what you're striving for), optimism has other benefits as well. So, if you want to achieve greater happiness, try being optimistic for a day.

Optimists enjoy a greater degree of academic success than pessimists do. Because optimistic students think it's possible for them to make a good grade, they study hardier and they study smarter. They manage the setting in which they study and they seek help from others when they need it. (Optimism, it turns out, is almost as predictive of how well students do in college as the SAT.)

Optimists are more self-confident than pessimists are. They believe in *themselves* more than fate.

Optimists are more likely to be problem-solvers than pessimists are. When pessimistic students get a D on a test, they tend to think things like: "I knew I shouldn't have taken this course. I'm no good at psychology." The optimistic student who gets a D says to herself, "I can do better. I just didn't study enough for this test. I'll do better next time." And she will.

Optimists welcome second chances after they fail more than pessimists do. Optimistic golfers always take a *mulligan* (a redo swing without penalty). Why? Because they expect to achieve a better result the second time around.

Optimists are more socially outgoing than pessimists are. Socially outgoing folks believe that the time they spend with other human beings makes them better in some way — smarter, more interesting, more attractive. Unfortunately, pessimists see little, if any, benefit from venturing out into the social world.

Optimists are not as lonely as pessimists are. Because pessimists don't see as much benefit from socializing with others, they have far fewer social and emotional connections in their lives, which is what loneliness is all about.

Optimists utilize social support more effectively than pessimists do. They aren't afraid to reach out in times of need.

Optimists are less likely to blame others for their misfortune than pessimists are. When you blame someone else for your troubles, what you're really saying is, "You're the *cause* of my problem and, therefore, you have to be the *solution* as well." Optimists have just as many troubles as pessimists throughout life — they just accept more responsibility for dealing with their misfortune.

Optimists cope with stress better than pessimists do. Pessimists worry, optimists act. A patient with coronary heart disease who is pessimistic "hopes and prays" that he doesn't have another heart attack anytime soon. The optimistic heart patient leaves little to chance — instead, he exercises regularly, practices his meditation exercises, adheres to a low-cholesterol diet, and makes sure he always gets a good night's sleep.

Chapter 3:

Happy People Use Their Character

Strengths

One of the most popular exercises in the science of positive psychology (some argue it is the single most popular exercise) is referred to as "use your signature strengths in new ways." But what does this exercise mean? How do you make the most of it to benefit yourself and others?

On the surface, the exercise is self-explanatory:

a. Select one of your highest strengths – one of your **character strengths** that is core to who you are, is easy for you to use, and gives you energy;

b. Consider a new way to express the strength each day;

c. Express the strength in a new way each day for at least 1 week.

Studies repeatedly show that this exercise is connected with long-term benefits (e.g., 6 months) such as higher levels of happiness and lower levels of depression.

PUT THE EXERCISE INTO PRACTICE

In practice, however, people sometimes find it surprisingly challenging to come up with new ways to use one of their signature strengths. This is because we are very accustomed to using our strengths. We frequently use our strengths mindlessly without much awareness. For example, have you paid much attention to your use of self-regulation as you brush your teeth? Your level of prudence or kindness while driving? Your humility while at a team meeting?

For some strengths, it is easy to come up with examples. Want to apply **curiosity** in a new way? Below is a sample mapping of what you might do. Keep it simple. Make it complex. It's up to you!

- On Monday, take a new route home from work and explore your environment as you drive.
- On Tuesday, ask one of your co-workers a question you have not previously asked them.
- On Wednesday, try a new food for lunch – something that piques your curiosity to taste.
- On Thursday, call a family member and explore their feelings about a recent positive experience they had.
- On Friday, take the stairs instead of the elevator and explore the environment as you do.
- On Saturday, as you do one household chore (e.g., washing the dishes, vacuuming), pay attention to 3 novel features of the activity while you do it. Example: Notice the whirring sound of the vacuum, the accumulation of dust swirling around in the container, the warmth of the water as you wash the dishes, the sensation of the weight of a single plate or cup, and so on.
- On Sunday, ask yourself 2 questions you want to explore about yourself – reflect or journal your immediate responses.
- Next Monday….keep going!

WIDENING THE SCOPE

In some instances, you might feel challenged to come up with examples. Let me help. After you choose one of your signature strengths, consider the following 10 areas to help jolt new ideas within you and stretch your approach to the strength.

How might I express the character strength…

- At work
- In my closest relationship
- While I engage in a hobby
- When with my friends
- When with my parents or children
- When I am alone at home
- When I am on a team
- As the leader of a project or group
- While I am driving
- While I am eating

Chapter 4:

Happy People Savor the

Moment

Learning to "savor the moment" in life is a convenient, free, and effective way to increase your happiness and quality of life and reduce stress. Enjoying what you have can help you to appreciate what you've got rather than lamenting what you don't have and creating stress by striving for too much. Being able to savor the moment with loved ones can bring a stronger connection and sense of appreciation, which leads to better quality relationships and all the benefits of social support that they bring. Learn more about these techniques to savor the moment in life.

1. Focus on Details

Sometimes as we go through life, we forget to stop and enjoy the little things; indeed, it's possible to go through an entire day either stuck in your ruminations about the past or anxious over the future, never really seizing the moment and noticing the pleasant things that are happening right now (and passing up positive opportunities right and left). As you savor the moment, notice the little things that can make a day special — the smile of a friend, the kindness of a stranger, the beauty of a sunset

2. Focus on Sensations

As you're experiencing your day, notice and memorize the details — especially the positive details — of what's happening around you. Create a memory. Notice the sounds you hear, like the sound of children's laughter in the background. Notice the smells, like the scent of a fresh sea breeze. And how did that wind feel on your face? Noticing these types of sensory details helps you live fully in the moment and can help evoke pleasant memories when you hear music, smell aroma, or feel sensations you experience on the days you want to savor.

3. Focus on the Positive

As humans, we're naturally wired to notice the negative events in life more than the positive, as these are what we need to keep track of to maintain our safety: if we're aware of threats around us, we're more able to launch a defense. However, if we actively focus on the positive, we can stress less and enjoy life more from an increasingly optimistic vantage point. To savor the moment, notice what's going right, and appreciate it. This isn't the same as pretending you're happy when you're not; it's more about noticing the things that lead to greater happiness and reduced stress.

4. Express Gratitude

Feeling gratitude goes along with noticing the positive and is an excellent way to savor the moment. Notice all the nice things that people do for you (and thank them whenever possible), or simply notice what you enjoy about people when they're just themselves (and be sure to tell them that, too). Appreciate what goes right in your day as it happens, and write it down in a gratitude journal at night — it's a surprisingly effective way to both raise your level of daily gratitude and build a record of all the things in your life that can make you happy when you're having a bad day.

Chapter 5:

What if You Treated Your Life

Like a Team Sport?

Here's something we can all agree on: we want our lives to matter. We all want to live a satisfying, fulfilling, and purposeful life.

This isn't just a selfish desire. I believe that feeling a certain amount of significance in your life is healthy. It's good for the human experience. There is a healthy satisfaction that comes from contributing to the world around you. It's important to your physical and mental health.

But there is a problem.

Simply saying, "You need to live a life of purpose" doesn't help anyone. It's too abstract. Sure, I want to live a life of purpose, fulfillment, and significance ... but how do I translate that into action? I certainly don't have all the answers. (Big surprise.) But here's one thing that has helped me recently: I've been thinking about my own life as a team sport. Viewing my life in this context has helped me develop a clear plan and design real action steps for living a healthier, happier, and more fulfilling life.

Here's how I'm thinking about my life as a team sport and how you might find it useful as well.

The Mission

Every team has a mission that it strives to accomplish. A good team measures itself by something: wins, losses, championships. There is no Superbowl of Life, but I like thinking about my life in the same way.

How do you want your life to be *measured*? What do you want to be counted? What is a win? What is a loss? Additionally, just as a team needs the effort of every teammate to fulfill its mission, you need the help of those around you to fulfill your mission. How will the people on your "team" help you get to where you want to go? What role do your family, friends, and peers play in helping you achieve these goals? What about your teachers, your boss, and your mentors?

So often, we think about big questions like, "What do I want to do with my life?" without considering everyone else that we live with. Thinking about your life as a team sport forces you to realize an important lesson: your life is dramatically impacted by the people around you.

Life is a shared experience. And for this reason, the people around you need to be part of the plan. A good mission in life is always about more than just you.

How I'm using this idea: I often think about the mission of our team (and the mission of my life) when it comes to what we are building here. I'm working to change how we approach our health and use the science of behavior change and habit formation to make it easier for us to live healthy lives. And to do it, I need the support of my family and friends, the guidance of mentors and business partners, and the help of readers like you. It may have started as my idea, but it rapidly became our mission.

Chapter 6:

<u>How to Eat With Mood in Mind</u>

At the point when you're feeling down, it tends to be enticing to go to food to lift your spirits. Notwithstanding, the sweet, fatty treats that numerous individuals resort to have unfortunate results of their own. Along these lines, you may puzzle over whether any good food sources can work on your temperament.

As of late, research on the connection between sustenance and psychological wellness has been arising. However, note that state of mind can be impacted by numerous variables, like pressure, climate, helpless rest, hereditary qualities, mood disorders, and nutritional deficiencies. In any case, certain food varieties have been displayed to further develop general mental wellbeing and specific kinds of temperament issues.

1. Fatty Fish

Omega-3 unsaturated fats are a gathering of fundamental fats you should get through your eating routine because your body can't produce them all alone. Fatty fish like salmon and tuna fish are wealthy in two sorts of omega-3s — docosahexaenoic corrosive (DHA) and eicosapentaenoic corrosive (EPA) — that are connected to bring down degrees of despair. Omega-3s add to lower your depression and seem to assume key parts in mental health and cell flagging.

2. Dark Chocolate

Chocolate is wealthy in numerous mood-boosting compounds. Its sugar may further develop mood since it's a fast wellspring of fuel for your brain. Besides, it's anything but a course of feel-great mixtures, like caffeine, theobromine, and N-acylethanolamine — a substance synthetically like cannabinoids that have been connected to improved mood.

3. Fermented Food Varieties

Fermented food sources, which incorporate kimchi, yogurt, kefir, fermented tea, and sauerkraut, may further develop gut wellbeing and state of mind. The fermentation interaction permits live microbes to flourish in food varieties ready to change over sugars into liquor and acids. During this interaction, probiotics are made. These live microorganisms support the development of solid microscopic organisms in your gut and may expand serotonin levels.

4. Bananas

Bananas may assist with flipping around a frown.

They're high in nutrient B6, which orchestrates feel-great synapses like dopamine and serotonin.

Moreover, one enormous banana (136 grams) gives 16 grams of sugar and 3.5 grams of fiber.

When matched with fiber, sugar is delivered gradually into your circulation system, considering stable glucose levels and better disposition control. Glucose levels that are too low may prompt irritability and emotional episodes.

5. Oats

Oats are an entire grain that can keep you feeling great the entire morning. You can appreciate them in numerous structures, like, for the time being, oats, oatmeal, muesli, and granola. They're a phenomenal wellspring of fiber, giving 8 grams in a solitary crude cup (81 grams). Fiber eases back your processing of carbs, considering a slow arrival of sugar into the circulation system to keep your energy levels stable.

Chapter 7:

How To Set Smart Goals

Setting your goals can be a tough choice. It's all about putting your priorities in such a way that you know what comes first for you. It's imperative to be goal-oriented to set positive goals for your present and future. You should be aware of your criteria for setting your goals. Make sure your plan is attainable in a proper time frame to get a good set of goals to be achieved in your time. You would need hard work and a good mindset for setting goals. Few components can help a person reach their destination. Control what you choose because it will eternally impact your life.

To set a goal to your priority, you need to know what exactly you want. In other words, be specific. Be specific in what matters to you and your goal. Make sure that you know your fair share of details about your idea, and then start working on it once you have set your mind to it. Get a clear vision of what your goal is. Get a clear idea of your objective. It is essential to give a specification to your plan to set it according to your needs.

Make sure you measure your goals. As in, calculate the profit or loss. Measure the risks you are taking and the benefits you can gain from them. In simple words, you need to quantify your goals to know what order to set them into. It makes you visualize the amount of time it will take or the energy to reach the finish line. That way, you can calculate your goals and their details. You need to set your mind on the positive technical growth of your goal. That is an essential step to take to put yourself to the next goal as soon as possible.

If you get your hopes high from the start, it may be possible that you will meet with disappointment along the way. So, it would be best if you made sure that your goals are realistic and achievable. Make sure your goal is within reach. That is the reality check you need to force in your mind that is your goal even attainable? Just make sure it is, and everything will go as planned. It doesn't mean to set small goals. There is a difference between big goals and unrealistic goals. Make sure to limit your romantic goals, or else you will never be satisfied with your achievement.

Be very serious when setting your goals, especially if they are long-term goals. They can impact your life in one way or another. It depends on you how you take it. Make sure your goals are relevant. So, that you can gain real benefit from your goals. Have your fair share of profits from your hard work and make it count. Always remember why the goal matters to you. Once you get the fundamental idea of why you need this goal to be achieved, you can look onto a bigger picture in the frame. If it doesn't feel relevant, then there is no reason for you to continue working for. Leave it as it is if it doesn't give you what you applied for because it will only drain your energy and won't give you a satisfactory outcome.

Time is an essential thing to keep in focus when working toward your goals. You don't want to keep working on one thing for too long or too short. So, keep a deadline. Keep a limit on when to work on your goal. If it's worth it, give it your good timer, but if not, then don't even waste a second on it. They are just some factors to set your goals for a better future. These visionary goals will help you get through most of the achievements you want to get done with.

Chapter 8:

8 Ways To Deal With Setbacks In Life

Life is never the same for anyone - It is an ever-changing phenomenon, making you go through all sorts of highs and lows. And as good times are an intrinsic part of your life, so are bad times. One day you might find yourself indebted by 3-digit figures while having only $40 in your savings account. Next day, you might be vacationing in Hawaii because you got a job that you like and pays $100,000 a year. There's absolutely no certainty to life (except passing away) and that's the beauty of it. You never know what is in store for you. But you have to keep living to see it for yourself. Setbacks in life cannot be avoided by anyone. Life will give you hardships, troubles, break ups, diabetes, unpaid bills, stuck toilet and so much more. It's all a part of your life.

Here's 8 ways that you might want to take notes of, for whenever you may find yourself in a difficult position in dealing with setback in life.

1. Accept and if possible, embrace it

The difference between accepting and embracing is that when you accept something, you only believe it to be, whether you agree or disagree. But when you embrace something, you truly KNOW it to be true and accept it as a whole. There is no dilemma or disagreement after you have embraced something.

So, when you find yourself in a difficult situation in life, accept it for what it is and make yourself whole-heartedly believe that this problem in your life, at this specific time, is a part of your life. This problem is what makes you complete. This problem is meant for you and only you can go through it. And you will. Period. There can be no other way.

The sooner you embrace your problem, the sooner you can fix it. Trying to bypass it will only add upon your headaches.

2. Learn from it

Seriously, I can't emphasize how important it is to LEARN from the setbacks you face in your life. Every hardship is a learning opportunity. The more you face challenges, the more you grow. Your capabilities expand with every issue you solve—every difficulty you go through, you rediscover yourself. And when you finally deal off with it, you are reborn. You are a new person with more wisdom and experience.

When you fail at something, try to explore why you failed. Be open-minded about scrutinizing yourself. Why couldn't you overcome a certain situation? Why do you think of this scenario as a 'setback'? The moment you find the answers to these questions is the moment you will have found the solution.

3. Execute What You Have Learnt

The only next step from here is to execute that solution and make sure that the next time you face a similar situation, you'll deal with it by having both your arms tied back and blindfolded. All you have to do is remember what you did in a similar past experience and reapply your previous solution.

Thomas A. Edison, the inventor of the light bulb, failed 10,000 times before finally making it. And he said "I have not failed. I just found 10,000 ways that won't work".

The lesson here is that you have to take every setback as a lesson, that's it.

4. Without shadow, you can never appreciate light

This metaphor is applicable to all things opposite in this universe. Everything has a reciprocal; without one, the other cannot exist. Just as without shadow, we wouldn't have known what light is, similarly, without light, we could've never known about shadow. The two opposites identify and complete each other.

Too much of philosophy class, but to sum it up, your problems in life, ironically, is exactly why you can enjoy your life. For example, if you are a chess player, then defeating other chess players will give you enjoyment while getting defeated will give you distress. But, when you are a chess prodigy—you have defeated every single chess player on earth and there's no one else to defeat, then what will you do to derive pleasure? Truth is, you can now no longer enjoy chess. You have no one to defeat. No one gives you the fear of losing anymore and as a result, the taste of winning has lost its appeal to you.

So, whenever you face a problem in life, appreciate it because without it, you can't enjoy the state of not having a problem. Problems give you the pleasure of learning from them and solving them.

5. View Every Obstacle As an opportunity

This one's especially for long term hindrances to your regular life. The COVID-19 pandemic for instance, has set us back for almost two years now. As distressing it is, there is also some positive impact of it. A long-term setback opens up a plethora of new avenues for you to explore. You suddenly get a large amount of time to experiment with things that you have never tried before.

When you have to pause a regular part of your life, you can do other things in the meantime. I believe that every one of us has a specific talent and most people never know what their talent is simply because they have never tried that thing.

6. Don't Be Afraid to experiment

People pursue their whole life for a job that they don't like and most of them never ever get good at it. As a result, their true talent gets buried under their own efforts. Life just carries on with unfound potential. But when some obstacle comes up and frees you from the clutches of doing what you have been doing for a long time, then you should get around and experiment. Who knows? You, a bored high school teacher, might be a natural at tennis. You won't know it unless you are fired from that job and actually play tennis to get over it. So whenever life gives you lemons, quit trying to hold on to it. Move on and try new things instead.

7. Stop Comparing yourself to others

The thing is, we humans are emotional beings. We become emotionally vulnerable when we are going through something that isn't supposed to be. And in such times, when we see other people doing fantastic things in life, it naturally makes us succumb to more self-loathing. We think lowly of our own selves and it is perfectly normal to feel this way. Talking and comapring ourselves to people who are seemingly untouched by setbacks is a counterproductive move. You will listen to their success-stories and get depressed—lose self-esteem. Even if they try their best to advise you, it won't get through to you. You won't be able to relate to them.

8. Talk to people other people who are having their own setbacks in life

I'm not asking you to talk to just any people. I'm being very specific here: talk to people who are going through bad times as well.

If you start talking to others who are struggling in life, perhaps more so compared to you, then you'll see that everyone else is also having difficulties in life. It will seem natural to you. Moreover, having talked with others might even show you that you are actually doing better than all these other people. You can always find someone who is dealing with more trouble than you and that will enlighten you. That will encourage you. If someone else can deal with tougher setbacks in life, why can't you?

Besides, listening to other people will give you a completely new perspective that you can use for yourself if you ever find yourself in a similar situation as others whom you have talked with.

Conclusion

Setbacks are a part of life. Without them we wouldn't know what the good times are. Without them we wouldn't appreciate the success that we have gotten. Without them we wouldn't cherish the moments that got us to where we are heading to. And without them there wouldn't be any challenge to fill our souls with passion and fire. Take setbacks as a natural process in the journey. Use it to fuel your drive. Use it to move your life forward one step at a time.

Chapter 9:

How to Learn Faster

Remember the saying, "You are never too old to learn something new"? Believe me, it's not true in any way you understood it.

The most reliable time to learn something new was the time when you were growing up. That was the time when your brain was in its most hyperactive state and could absorb anything you had thrown at it.

You can still learn, but you would have to change your approach to learning.

You won't learn everything, because you don't like everything going on around you. You naturally have an ego to please. So what can you do to boost your learning? Let's simplify the process. When you decide to learn something, take a moment and ask yourself this; "Will this thing make my life better? Will this fulfill my dreams? Will I benefit from it?".

If you can answer all these questions in a positive, you will pounce on the thing and you won't find anyone more motivated than you.

Learning is your brain's capability to process things constructively. If you pick up a career, you won't find it hard to flourish if you are genuinely interested in that particular skill.

Whether it be sports, singing, entrepreneurship, cooking, writing, or anything you want to pursue. Just ask yourself, can you use it to increase your creativity, your passion, your satisfaction. If you can, you will start learning it as if you knew it all along.

Your next step to learning faster would be to improve and excel at what you already have. How can you do that? It's simple yet again!

Ask yourself another question, that; "Why must I do this? Why do I need this?" if you get to answer that, you will find the fastest and effective way to the top yourself without any coaching. Why will this happen on its own? Because now you have found a purpose for your craft and the destination is clear as the bright sun in the sky.

The last but the most important thing to have a head start on your journey of learning is the simplest of them all, but the hardest to opt for. The most important step is to start working towards things.

The flow of learning is from Head to Heart to Hands. You have thought of the things you want to do in your brain. Then you asked your heart if it satisfied you. Now it's time to put your hands to work.

You never learn until you get the chance to experience the world yourself. When you go through a certain event, your brain starts to process the outcomes that could have been, and your heart tells you to give it one more try. Here is the deciding moment. If you listen to your heart right away, you will get on a path of learning that you have never seen before.

What remains now is your will to do what you have decided. And when you get going, you will find the most useful resources immediately. Use your instincts and capitalize your time. Capture every chance with sheer will and belief as if this is your final moment for your dreams to come true.

It doesn't matter if you are not the ace in the pack, it doesn't matter if you are not in your peak physical shape, it doesn't matter if you don't have the money yet. You will someday get all those things only if you had the right skills and the right moment.

For all you know, this moment right now is the most worth it moment. So don't go fishing in other tanks when you have your own aquarium. That aquarium is your body, mind, and soul. All you need is to dive deep with sheer determination and the stars are your limit.

Chapter 10:

Becoming High Achievers

By becoming high achievers we become high off life, what better feeling is there than aiming for something you thought was unrealistic and then actually hitting that goal.

What better feeling is there than declaring we will do something against the perceived odds and then actually doing it.

To be a high achiever you must be a believer,

You must believe in yourself and believe that dream is possible for you.

It doesn't matter what anyone else thinks , as long as you believe,

To be a high achiever we must hunger to achieve.

To be an action taker.

Moving forward no matter what.

High achievers do not quit.

Keeping that vision in their minds eye until it becomes reality, no matter what.

Your biggest dream is protected by fear , loss and pain.

We must conquer all 3 of these impostors to walk through the door.

Not many do , most are still fighting fear and if they lose the battle, they quit.

Loss and pain are part of life.

Losses are hard on all of us.

Whether we lose possessions, whether we lose friends, whether we lose our jobs, or whether we lose family members.

Losing doesn't mean you have lost.

Losses are may be a tough pill to swallow, but they are essential because we cannot truly succeed until we fail.

We can't have the perfect relationship if we stay in a toxic one, and we can't have the life we desire until we make room by letting go of the old.

The 3 imposters that cause us so much terror are actually the first signs of our success.

So walk through fear in courage , look at loss as an eventual gain, and know that the pain is part of the game and without it you would be weak.

Becoming a high achiever requires a single minded focus on your goal, full commitment and an unnatural amount of persistence and work.

We must define what high achievement means to us individually, set the bar high and accept nothing less.

The achievement should not be money as money is not our currency but a tool.

The real currency is time and your result is the time you get to experience the world's places and products , so the result should always be that.

The holiday home , the fast car and the lifestyle of being healthy and wealthy, those are merely motivations to work towards. Like Carrots on a stick.

High achievement is individual to all of us, it means different things to each of us,

But if we are going to go for it we might as well go all out for the life we want, should we not?

I don't think we beat the odds of 1 in 400 trillion to be born, just to settle for mediocrity, did we?

Being a high achiever is in your DNA , if you can beat the odds , you can beat anything.

It is all about self-belief and confidence, we must have the confidence to take the action required and often the risk.

Risk is difficult for people and it's a difficult tight rope to walk. The line between risk and recklessness is razor thin.

Taking risks feels unnatural, not surprisingly as we all grew up in a health and safety bubble with all advice pointing towards safe and secure ways.

But the reward is often in the risk and sometimes a leap of blind faith is required. This is what stops most of us - the fear of the unknown.

The truth is the path to success is foggy and we can only ever see one step ahead , we have to imagine the result and know it's somewhere down this foggy path and keep moving forward with our new life in mind.

Know that we can make it but be aware that along the path we will be met by fear , loss and pain and the bigger our goal the bigger these monsters will be.

The top achievers financially are fanatical about their work and often work 100+ hours per week.

Some often work day and night until a project is successful.

Being a high achiever requires giving more than what is expected, standing out for the high standard of your work because being known as number 1 in your field will pay you abundantly.

Being an innovator, thinking outside the box for better practices, creating superior products to your competition because quality is more rewarding than quantity.

Maximizing the quality of your products and services to give assurance to your customers that your company is the number 1 choice.

What can we do differently to bring a better result to the table and a better experience for our customers?

We must think about questions like that because change is inevitable and without thinking like that we get left behind, but if we keep asking that, we can successfully ride the wave of change straight to the beach of our desired results.

The route to your success is by making people happy because none of us can do anything alone, we must earn the money and to earn it we must make either our employers or employees and customers happy.

To engage in self-promotion and positive interaction with those around us, we must be polite and positive with everyone, even with our competition.

Because really the only competition is ourselves and that is all we should focus on.

Self-mastery, how can I do better than yesterday?

What can I do different today that will improve my circumstances for tomorrow.

Little changes add up to a big one.

The belief and persistence towards your desired results should be 100%, I will carry on until… is the right attitude.

We must declare to ourselves that we will do this , we don't yet know how but we know that we will.

Because high achievers like yourselves know that to make it you must endure and persist untill you win.

High achievers have an unnatural grit and thick skin , often doing what others won't, putting in the extra hours when others don't.

After you endure loss and conquer pain , the sky is the limit, and high achievers never settle until they are finished.

Chapter 11:

5 Ways Quitting Something Can Bring You Joy

Do you ever wonder if you will ever be truly happy in your life? Do you wonder if happiness is just a hoax and success is an illusion? Do you feel like they don't exist? I know a friend who felt like this a little while ago. At the time, she was making a six-figure income, was working for her dream company (Apple), and had a flexible work schedule. Despite all this, she was miserable. She would have never been able to quit my job if not for the practice she got from quitting little things.

Of all the things that she tried, quitting these seven little things made her the happiest.

1. Quit Reading the News

News headlines are usually about happenings around the world. Most times, they are negative. Negative headlines make for better stories than positive headlines. Would you read a headline that says 'Electric Chair Makes a Comeback' or a headline that says 'Legislation debate in Tennessee'? See what I mean.

Journalists have to write stories that interest us. I can't blame them for that. Changing the time that I caught up on the news helped me be more positive during the day. Start reading inspirational posts first thing in the morning instead of news. You can still catch the news later, around 11 am instead of at 6 am.

2. Quit Hunching Your Shoulders

This boosted my confidence levels.

We hunch our shoulders and take up as little space as possible when we feel nervous and not too comfortable. This is body language 101.

Keeping a posture, opening up your shoulders will make you feel more confident during the day. But, I must admit it will make you more tired than usual. It will take you at least a total of 45 days before you start doing this effortlessly.

3. Quit Keeping a Corporate Face at Work

We are all trained not to show real feelings at work. Having a corporate face is good for corporate, not for you. Smiling all day, even when you are upset, will lift your mood. It will make you feel better sooner. Studies have shown that smiling makes you happy.

4. Quit Writing Huge Goals

It is better to write and work towards achievable goals before starting to write our stretch goals. Stretch goals are great to push ourselves. But, we all need achievable goals to boost confidence and to have successes that we can build momentum on. This can be hard for you if you are an overachiever.

Fries are comfort food for a lot of people. But eating them saps energy.

Eat oranges instead of fries every time you feel down and feel the need for comfort food. This not only boosts your energy but will also help you lose some pounds if you want to. Plus, this will give you energy and clarity of mind.

Chapter 12:

"Happy People Enjoy the Hidden Pleasures life has to offer."

It is said that the best things in your life are free, and there is not even a shred of doubt in that life is filled with satisfying hidden pleasures. To feel fulfilled, you need to enjoy them, so we are going to list some of the most simple, satisfying hidden pleasures life has to offer so that next time when you find yourself in a similar situation, you take out a moment and truly enjoy it:

Finding money you did not know you had: Reaching into your pocket and finding out a dollar 20 bill from the last time you went out wearing those jeans brings absolute joy all of a sudden. You have some extra money on you that you completely forgot about.

Receiving a Real letter via snail mail: Since email is more used these days, it has become the primary source of written communication, and most of the things you find in your snail mail are junk. So, when you find a package or a letter from someone you know in the mail, it brings joy, and a sense of excitement takes over you as you start opening the gift.

Making Brief Eye Contact with Someone of the Opposite Sex: We are all so busy in our lives, and most of the times when we are out, we spend time looking at our screens, so sometimes there is a rare moment where you pass them in a subway or street, and they look at you momentarily making direct eye contact that communicates a subtle curiosity, and for a second you think about it and then it's just gone.

Saying the Same Thing Simultaneously: Sometimes, you and your friend notice something or react to something by yelling out the same set of words. This is something that occurs rarely, but it gives you something to smile about.

Realizing You Have More Time to Sleep: Sometimes, you abruptly wake up in the middle of the night, and you think it's time to wake up, and when you look at the time, and you still have two more hours to sleep. A warm euphoric feeling shoots through your body at that moment, and then you glide back to your dreams.

The feeling after a healthy workout: There is a feeling of self-satisfaction and accomplishment that you get; this is one activity that will make you feel better and also make you look good at the same time. So when you walk out of the main door of the gym, you feel like you are on top of the world.

Relaxing Outdoors on a Sunny Day: When you are relaxing in your chair, reading your favourite book as the light breeze keeps the temperature under control, and the sun warms your skin, you feel at peace with the environment around you.

Making Someone smile: Sometimes you notice that your fellow student is under great stress due to the exams that are just coming up, so you invite them over to your place to just relax, have good food and watch a movie with a smile on their face as they enjoy yourself will make you the happiest.

Chapter 13:

<u>Seven Habits That Will Make You</u>

<u>Successful</u>

A man's habits are as good as his lifestyle. Some habits are akin to successful people. The path to greatness is less traveled and the habits to success may be difficult for some people to sustain.

The road to success is narrow and occasionally thorny because habits that will make you successful are uncomfortable and difficult to adapt. Similar to Charles Darwin's theory of survival for the fittest, only those who manage to trim their excesses and shape their habits will eventually be successful.

Here are seven habits that will make you successful:

1. <u>Integrity</u>

Integrity is one of the measures of success. It is the ability to live an honest life free from swindling, blackmail, and corruption among other vices. Integrity is the morality of a person and is relative from one person to another. However, there is a generally accepted threshold of integrity expected of people in different social, political, and economic classes.

Integrity is uncommon to most people making it highly valuable. People will forget how you looked but will never forget how you made them feel. Integrity holds back one from committing such awful mistakes. It will help you award the deserving, condemn vices, be intolerable to corruption, and make transparency your middle name.

The lack of integrity is responsible for the downfall of great people and business empires. Political leaders worldwide have lost their crown of glory to corruption. They were once the dream of every pupil in school and aspiring young leaders looked up to them. Corruption and greed stole that from them.

So powerful is integrity that successful people guard theirs' tooth and nail. Once eroded, their success is at stake. It may crumble down like a mound hill. Do you want to be successful? Have integrity.

2. <u>An Open Mind</u>

It is the ability to tolerate and be receptive to divergent ideas different from your beliefs. It takes a lot to accommodate the opinions of others and accept their reasoning to be rational. Successful people fully understand that they do not have a monopoly on brilliant ideas. As such, they cautiously welcome the proposals of other people while allowing room for further advancement.

Entertaining the ideas of other people does not mean blindly accepting them. It is the habit of successful people to be critical of everything, balancing their options and only settling for the best. An open mind translates to an analytical and inquisitive nature. The zeal to venture into the unknown and experiment with new waters.

Successful people are distinguished from others because they challenge the status quo. They seek to improve their best and develop alternatives to the existing routines. The reason why they are successful in the first place is their open mind.

How does one have an open mind? It is by being open to infinite possibilities of a hundred and one ways of approaching issues. Routine is an enemy of open-mindedness and by extension, success. It is of course inevitable not to follow a routine at our places of work, schools, or families. It is acceptable to that extent. Being its slave is completely unacceptable.

3. Move With Time

Time is never stagnant. The world evolves around time and seasons. The wise is he who deciphers and interprets them correctly. The measure of success in these modern times is different from those in the ancient days. A lot has changed.

In this era of technological advancements, we cannot afford to live in analog ways. The poor readers of seasons are stagnant in one position for a long time. Success is elusive in their hands. A look at business giants will reveal their mastery of times and seasons. They do not fumble at it. Not one bit.

Successful businesses deal with tools of the trade of the modern world. From the great Microsoft corporation to the Coca-cola company. All of them align themselves with the market demand presently. Learning the present time and season is a habit that will elevate you to success.

4. Learn From The Mistakes of Others

It is prudent to learn from the mistakes of other people and not from yours. Keenly observe those ahead of you and watch out not to fall into their traps. It is regretful to be unable to take a cue from our predecessors and learn from their failures.

Successful people travel down roads once taken (for the advantage of hindsight) by others – except for a few adventurous ones who venture into the unknown. The benefit of hindsight is very important because we learn from the mistakes of those who preceded us and adjust accordingly. Develop a habit of watching closely those ahead of you and take a cue from them not to commit similar mistakes. This habit will propel you to the doorstep of success.

5. Investment Culture

It is prudent to be mindful of tomorrow. No amount of investment is too little. Successful people do not consume everything they produce. They save a portion of their income for the future. Investment is a culture developed over time. Some people find it difficult to postpone the entire consumption of their income. They will only settle when nothing is left. This is retrogressive.

An investment culture curbs wastage and emphasizes tomorrow's welfare. Moreover, to reduce risk, the investment portfolio is diversified. It is dangerous to risk everything in one endeavor. Captains of industries worldwide have invested broadly in different sectors. This makes them stay afloat even during tough economic seasons.

6. Choosing Your Battles

On your way to success, do not make many enemies. This habit is ancient but very relevant to date. Unnecessary fights will wear you out and divert you away from the goal. Petty distractions will hijack your focus and successfully make you unsuccessful.

Learn to train your guns on things that matter. Feed your focus and starve your fears. Ignore useless petty issues that may lead to tainting of your public image. Fight your battles wisely.

7. <u>Learn To Listen</u>

Listening is an art beyond hearing. It is paying detailed attention to the speech of others, both verbal and non-verbal. Always listen more and talk less – a common argument for having two ears and one mouth. To be successful, you will have to pay closer attention to what is unspoken. Listen to the way people communicate. You will pick up genuine intentions in their speech and align yourself accordingly.

Once perfected, these seven habits will make you successful.

Chapter 14:

<u>10 Habits of Bernard Arnault</u>

Bernard Arnault- French investor, businessman, and CEO of LVMH recently reclaimed the title "worlds' wealthiest" from fellow billionaire Jeff Bezos. His business acumen and awe-inspiring financial achievements deserve to be recognized. His perspective can serve as a model for entrepreneurs who want to follow in his footsteps.

Bernard Arnault has written about money, prosperity, leadership, and power over the years. Moreover, his path to becoming the CEO of one of the world's most recognized brands will provide you with valuable lessons to emulate from. That is, your life circumstances shouldn't stop you from expanding and thriving outside your expertise.

Following his impressive accomplishments, here are ten points you can take away from Arnault's journey to success.

1. Happiness Before Money

According to Bernard, happiness is leading. That is leading your team to the top whether you are in business, sports, music industry. Money, according to him, is a consequence, and success is a blend of your past and future.

Your priority is not what you'll make sooner! When you put much-required effort into your job, profits will flow.

2. Mistakes Your Lesson

Your biggest mistake is your learning opportunity. When your business isn't performing well, understand the situation first and be patient.

In the world of innovative brands, it can take years to get something to work. Give it time and put yourself in a long-term expectation.

3. Always Behave as a Startup

Think small. Act quickly. Smaller boats can turn faster than more giant tankers. Arnault emphasizes the significance of thinking small. LVMH, in Arnault's opinion, is not a massive corporation device with miles of unnecessary bureaucracy.

Believe in your vision while attracting the best talent for your success path. A handy, adaptable speed, one that can fail quickly as easy to sleeve up.

4. Continuously Reinvent Yourself

How do you maintain your relevance? Bernard's LVMH is built on innovation, quality, entrepreneurship, and, essentially, on long-term vision. LVMH excels at developing increasingly desirable new products and selling them globally.

To be successful today, with your capabilities, opt for a worldwide startup and see what's going on. This necessitates a more considerable investment, which gives you an advantage. However, let the Creators run your inventions.

5. Team-Creative Control

Arnault strategies find creative control under each product's team to do what they do best. Arnault's designers are the dreamer's realists and critics. Allow your team to take creative control. You risk putting a tourniquet around their minds if you restrict them in any way.

6. Create Value To Attract Customers

Marketing investigates what the customer desires. As a result, you are doing what they need: creating a product and testing it to see if it works. Keeping your products in close contact with consumers, according to Arnault, makes a desire to buy in them. LVMH creates products that generate customers. For him, it's never about sales; it's always about creating desire. Your goal should be to be desirable for long-term marketability.

7. Trust the Process

There will always be different voices in business, and while there will undoubtedly be good advice, if you believe an idea will succeed, you may need to persevere until the end. Like Arnault, disregard your critics by following through with your vision to excel.

8. Your Persistence Is Everything

It would be best if you were very persistent. It would be best to have ideas, but the idea is only 20% of the equation. The execution rate is 80%. So if you are trying out a startup, having ideas marvellous, the driving force is persistence and execution.

When it comes to the most successful startups, such as Facebook, the idea was great from the beginning. Others, however, had the same idea. So why is Facebook such a phenomenal success today? It is critically through execution with persistence.

9. Do Not Think of Yourself

Bernard Arnault can be differentiated from other billionaires like Elon Musk or Bill Gates by focusing on the brands, making their longevity rather than making himself the face. He is only concerned with promoting his products.

To accomplish this, you must maintain contact with pioneers and designers, for example, while also making their ideas more specific and sustainable.

10. Maintain Contact With Your Company

One of the most common leadership mistakes is to lose sight of the company once you reach the top and "stick" with manageable goals. Instead, to see if the machine is working correctly or if there is room for improvement, you must examine every corner and every part of it.

Conclusion

Your willingness to outwork and your ability to outlearn everyone will keep your success journey intact and going. Bernard Arnault's path to becoming the CEO of the worlds most recognized and desired multi-billion empire of brands have a valuable lesson for you: your starting point does not influence or determine your future destination.

Chapter 15:

Happy People Give Freely

"For it is in giving that we receive." - Saint Francis of Assisi.

A Chinese saying goes by, "If you want happiness for an hour, take a nap. If you want happiness for a day, go fishing. If you want happiness for a year, inherit a fortune. If you want happiness for a lifetime, help somebody." It is indeed better to give than to receive. Scientific research provides compelling anecdotal evidence that giving is a powerful pathway to personal growth and lasting happiness. When we give freely, our brain stimulates endorphins and blesses us with a feeling of euphoria. Altruism is hardwired in our brains and tends to provide us with pleasure. Helping others is a secret to living a happier and healthier, wealthier, productive, and more meaningful life.

Whether it's a charity, a piece of advice, a helping hand of any sort, or supporting someone throughout their journey, researchers Dunn, Aknin, Akin, and Norton performed a study. They showed that there is, in fact, a link between generosity and happier life. The gesture of caring about other people and doing something to improve their quality of life is the source of happiness. Once you start giving, you will feel more content and happier, and there will be no going back. You will get addicted to helping others and to the feeling that follows.

A group of psychologists from the University of California Santa Barbara conducted a study to ascertain if generosity is part of human nature. The observation showed that being a giver is more fulfilling than being a receiver and that generosity is deeply embedded in our systems. "You don't need to become a self-sacrificing martyr to feel happier. Just being a little more generous will suffice," says Prof. Tobler.

High-generosity respondents appeared not only happier but happier more often. This overarching sense of happiness in high-generosity individuals may positively affect their higher likelihood of finding life more meaningful. They were also 20% more likely to be optimistic about their future, be proud of themselves, and find enjoyment in their jobs. It's no secret that you have to give a little to get a little. The more generous you are too loved ones, acquaintances, or even strangers, the more likely those selfless deeds will be reciprocated sometime down the line. Neuroeconomics found in a recent study that merely promising to be more generous is enough to trigger a change in our brain that will eventually make us happier.

In a 2006 study, Jorge Moll and colleagues at the National Institutes of Health found that when people give, it could be anything; it activates the warm glow effect, regions of the brain associated with pleasure, social connection, and trust. Whatever you are giving to people, society, or nature, you will find yourself benefiting from a hefty dose of happiness in the process. When you express your gratitude in words or actions, you not only boost your positivity but other people's as well. The more we give, the more we stand to gain purpose, meaning, and happiness – all of the things we look for in life but are so hard to find.

Chapter 16:

6 Tricks To Become More Aware Of Your Strengths

"Strength and growth come only through continuous effort and struggle." - Napoleon Hill.

While it is true that we tend to focus more on our weaknesses than on our strengths, it is also true that we should polish our strengths more than our weaknesses. This in no way means that we should consider ourselves superior to others and start looking away from that we have flaws. Unfortunately, most of us don't spend much time on self-reflection and self-awareness. But they are the vital aspects if we are thinking of improving ourselves in any way.

Here are 6 Tricks to become more aware of your strengths:

1. Decide to be more self-aware

Human beings are complicated creatures. Our minds are designed so that we tend to absorb more negative than positive thoughts about ourselves and others. For this reason, self-awareness is perhaps the most crucial thing in an individual's life. Self-awareness is the ability to look deep inside of yourself and monitor your emotions and reactions. It is the ability to allow yourself to be aware of your strengths, weaknesses, as well as your triggers, motivators, and other characteristics. We'll help you find a set of tricks and techniques that you can apply to polish your strengths in a self-awareness way; and how to use your strengths in a promising way.

2. Meditation:

The first thought that will come to your mind would be, "Is this person crazy? How can meditation help us improve our strengths?" But hear me out. The fresh breeze of the morning when everything is at peace, and you sit there inhaling all the good energy in and the bad energy out, your mind and thoughts would automatically become slow-paced and calm. Once you get to relax with yourself, you can analyze the things that have been happening in your life and develop possible solutions on how you can deal with them using your strengths. The positive energy and calming mood you will get after meditating would help you make your decisions wisely when you are under pressure and your mind is in chaos.

3. Labelling your thoughts:

More often, our thoughts reflect on our behavior and what makes us fail or succeed in life. People can genuinely relate to a situation where they could have possibly thought about a worst-case scenario, but in the end, nothing as such happened. Our anxiety and hopelessness don't come from the situation we are struggling with, but rather our thoughts make us believe in the worst possible things that could happen to us. But we're stronger than we give ourselves credit for. We have the power to control our negative thoughts and turn them into positive ones. We can list all the ideas and thinking that provide us with stress and tension and then label them as either useful or useless. If the particular thought is causing a significant effect in your life, you can work towards it to make your life better and less anxious. Know your priorities and take help from your strengths to tackle the problems.

4. **Befriending your fears:**

There's not a single person on this planet who isn't afraid of something. Be it the fear of losing your loved ones or any phobias of either animal, insects, heights, closed spaces, etc. There are also so many fears related to our self-worth and whether we are good enough, skilled enough, or deserving enough of anything. To accept these fears and work towards overcoming them is perhaps the most powerful thing one could do. It takes so much of a person's strength and willpower to befriend fear, reduce it, and finally eliminate it. Most of the time, we end up in situations that we always feared, and then we have to take quick actions and make wise decisions. To remain calm in such cases and use your strengths and experiences to tackle whatever's in front of you is a remarkable quality found in only a few. But we can also achieve and polish this quality by strengthening our minds and preparing ourselves to get us out of situations wisely and effectively. To be patient and look into the problems from every angle is the critical component of this one.

5. **Watching your own movie:**

Narrating your life experiences to yourself or a close friend and telling yourself and them how far you have come can boost your self-confidence immensely. You should go in flashbacks and try to remember all the details of your life. You will find that there were some moments you felt immense joy and some moments where you felt like giving up. But with all the strength that you were collecting along the way, you endured the possible tortures and struggles and challenges and eventually rose again. So you should focus and be well aware of how you tackle those situations, what powers you have, and the strengths that couldn't let you give up but face everything. Once you have found the answers to the above questions, like for example, it was your patience and bravery that helped you through it, or it was your wise and speedy decisions that made it all effective, you can understand what strengths you have and make use of them later in life too.

6. Motivate yourself:

We should stop looking for others to notice how great we did or stop waiting for a round of applause or a pat on the back from them. Instead, we should motivate ourselves every time we fall apart, and we should have the energy to pick ourselves back up again. The feeling of satisfaction we get after completing a task or helping someone, that feeling is what we should strive for. We should become proud of ourselves and our strengths, as well as our weaknesses, that they helped us transform into the person we are today. We should never feel either superior or inferior to others. Everyone has their own pace and their own struggles. Our strengths should not only be for ourselves but for others too. Kindness, empathy, hospitality, being there for people, patience, courage, respect are all the qualities that one must turn into their strengths.

Conclusion:

The key to perfection is self-awareness. There's a fine line between who you are and who you strive to become; it can be achieved by becoming aware of your strengths, polishing them, and creating a sense of professional as well as personal development. Your strengths motivate you to try new things, achieve new skills, become a better version of yourself. Your strengths are what keeps you positive, motivated, help you to maintain your stress better, aid you in your intuitive decision making, and command you to help others as well. It inspires you to become a better person.

Chapter 17:

Five Habits For An Extremely
Productive Day

Our productivity and efficiency during the day are variables of several factors. Some days seem better, the sun a little brighter than normal; the food tastes sweeter and the mood lighter. In such days, unmatched joy bubbles within us increasing our productivity exponentially. Many people cannot choose when to experience these days. Instead, they are at the mercy of their emotions and the influence of other people who can ruin their day whenever they please.

Here are five habits for an extremely productive day:

1. Plan For Your Day Beforehand.

Failure to plan is planning to fail. A plan is an integral part of success. It means that you understand the obligation you have to live the day ahead and the duties and responsibilities in your in-tray. A plan will help you check all the boxes on your to-do list and you can track your progress in each.

In planning for your day, you will know the resources that you have and those that you lack. It is also possible to budget on your means earlier rather than waiting for the actual day and start scampering for resources. A wise man does not live on a borrowed budget but within his own.

A good plan is a job half done. Your day will be more productive when nothing takes you by surprise because you would have anticipated every occurrence beforehand and it will find you armed with a solution.

2. Wake Up Early

The early bird catches the worm. Punctuality is very important if you want to have a productive day. An early riser has a fresh and clear mind compared to those who wake up late and start their routine fast because they are behind schedule. They do not have the advantage of calmness and composure because they want to make up for time lost. This exposes them to error and ridicule from their enemies if they fail, which is imminent because of their inaccuracy.

When one wakes up early, one has an advantage over other people. They can open their businesses or start their work earlier than their competitors do. They maximize their productivity because they have created enough time for each task they had scheduled. Consider waking up early to have an extremely productive day.

3. Do Not Bite More Than You Can Chew

This calls for sobriety in the handling of tasks and designing of goals. The pressure to outdo yourself can be overwhelming enough to make you lose focus on what is at stake. It is paramount to set realistic and achievable goals so that you can concentrate on them. Shun anything that presents itself to you that is beyond your ability no matter how attractive it seems.

The power of self-control is at play. Resist the temptation of going out of your way to prove a point for the sake of it. Instead, fully concentrate on what you had planned. Schedule anything outside your plan to the following day. It is far from procrastination because in this case, you have a clearly defined timeline on when to actualize your plans.

Failure to develop this habit will lead you to a situation where you have many unfinished tasks. This is not productivity, by all standards. Focus on what you can manage and do it efficiently.

4. Avoid Negative Company

A negative company will derail your progress and work. When you associate yourself with such people, you will not see the unseen benefit in challenges and instead, you will focus on the undone, incomplete, and failed bits of your work. Failure is contagious. If you constantly surround yourself with a clique of failures, you too shall fail.

To have a productive day, have friends who share your vision. You will blossom under their shade and they will encourage you in your work. This will show you possibility even when you see failure and doom. In their company, your days will be productive and joyful.

5. Look At The Bigger Picture

As you seek to have productive days, look at the bigger picture. It will make you focus on the greater plan you have rather than petty squabbles and meaningless distractions that come your way. The bigger picture will always remind you of your cause and inspire you to live up to it even when challenges come your way.

When you pay attention to the above five habits, you will have extremely productive days. It all lies in your effort to adopt them.

Chapter 18:

6 Steps To Focus On Growth

Growth is a lifelong process. We grow every moment from the day we are born until our eventual death. And the amazing thing about growth is that there is no real limit to it.

Now, what exactly is growth? Well, growing is the process of changing from one state to another and usually, it has to be positive; constructive; better-than-before. Although growth occurs equally towards all directions in the early years of our life, the rate of growth becomes more and more narrowed down to only a few particular aspects of our life as we become old. We become more distinctified as individuals, and due to our individuality, not everyone of us can possibly grow in all directions. With our individual personality, experiences, characteristics, our areas of growth become unique to us. Consequently, our chances of becoming successful in life corresponds to how we identify our areas of growth and beam them on to our activities with precision. Let us explore some ways to identify our key areas of growth and utilize them for the better of our life.

1. Identify Where You Can Grow

For a human being, growth is relative. One person cannot grow in every possible way because that's how humans are—we simply cannot do every thing at once. One person may grow in one way while another may grow in a completely different way. Areas of growth can be so unlike that one's positive growth might even seem like negative growth to another person's perspective. So, it is essential that we identify the prime areas where we need to grow. This can be done through taking surveys, asking people or critically analyzing oneself. Find out what lackings do you have as a human being, find out what others think that you lack as a human being. Do different things and note down where you are weak but you have to do it anyway. Then, make a list of those areas where you need growing and move on to the next step.

2. Accept That You Need To Grow In Certain Areas

After carefully identifying your lackings, accept these in your conscious and subconscious mind. Repeatedly admit to yourself and others that you lack so and so qualities where you wish to grow with time.

Never feel ashamed of your shortcomings. Embrace them comfortably because you cannot trully change yourself without accepting that you need to change. Growth is a dynamic change that drags you way out of your comfort zone and pushes you into the wild. And to start on this endeavor for growth, you need to have courage. Growth is a choice that requires acceptance and humility.

3. Remind Yourself of Your Shortcomings

You can either write it down and stick it on your fridge or just talk about it in front of people you've just met—this way, you'll constantly keep reminding yourself that you have to grow out of your lackings. And this remembrance will tell you to try—try improving little by little. Try growing.

It is important to remain consciously aware of these at all times because you never know when you might have to face what. All the little and big things you encounter every day are all opportunities of growth. This takes us to the fourth step:

4. Face Your Problems

Whatever you encounter, in any moment or place in your life is an opportunity created: an opportunity for learning. A very old adage goes: "the more we learn, the more we grow". So, if you don't face your problems and run away from them, then you are just losing the opportunity to learn from it, and thus, losing the opportunity of growing from it. Therefore, facing whatever life throws at you also has an important implication on your overall growth. Try to make yourself useful against all odds. Even if you fail at it, you will grow anyway.

5. Cross The Boundary

So, by now you have successfully identified your areas of growth, you have accepted them, you constantly try to remind yourself of them and you face everything that comes up, head on—never running away. You are already making progress. Now comes the step where you push yourself beyond your current status. You go out of what you are already facing and make yourself appear before even more unsettling circumstances.

This is a very difficult process, but if you grow out of here, nothing can stop you ever. And only a few people successfully make it through. You create your own problems, no one might support you and yet still, you try to push forward, make yourself overcome new heights of difficulties and grow like the tallest tree in the forest. You stand out of the crowd. This can only be done in one or two subjects in a lifetime. So make sure that you know where you want to grow. Where you want to invest that much effort, and time, and dedication. Then, give everything to it. Growth is a life's journey.

6. Embrace Your Growth

After you have crossed the boundary, there is no turning back. You have achieved new heights in your life, beyond what you thought you could have ever done. The area—the subject in which you tried to develop yourself, you have made yourself uniquely specialized in that particular area. You have outgrown the others in that field. It is time for you to make yourself habituated with that and embrace it gracefully. The wisdom you've accumulated through growth is invaluable—it has its roots deeply penetrated into your life. The journey that you've gone through while pursuing your growth will now define you. It is who you are.

As I've mentioned in the first line, "growth is a lifelong process". Growth is not a walk in the park, It is you tracking through rough terrains—steep heights and unexplored depths for an entire lifetime. Follow these simple yet difficult steps; grow into the tallest tree and your life will shine upon you like the graceful summer sun.

Chapter 19:

How to Determine What Makes You Happy

Finding your happiness is an art, not science, but here are five things I've done to help me figure where my happiness is coming from.

1. Wipe Your Happiness Slate Clean

If you're a human who is alive, the society you grew up in has Ideas about what happiness looks like. These ideas have permeated our lives since the moment we could understand shapes and colors; they've wormed their way into our soft, sweet subconsciouses.

On some level, most of us believe we will be happier when:

- We are thinner than we are now

- We earn more money

- We live in a bigger, prettier, better-located home

- We have more friends

- We're in a committed romantic relationship

And maybe some of those things really will make us happier! Supportive relationships and aerobic activity have been shown to reduce depression.

I imagine moving into a space with more natural light, and a shorter commute wouldn't hurt anything, either.

But for the sake of this experiment, let's do our very, very best to let go of preconceived notions about what makes us happy. Let's forget what our families and friends believe happiness looks like. Let's view this as a grand experiment with totally unknown results. Who knows what we'll discover!

P.S. Don't get down on yourself for "buying into cultural expectations of happiness." We all do it. We're not robots. For Pete's sake, Oprah's been trying to diet her way to happiness for two decades.

2. Start Taking Detailed Notes When You Feel Really Happy

Do you know those moments of "*If this isn't nice, I don't know what is*"? Those moments when you'd lift your face to the sky and grin (but you don't because it feels awkward), make a note of *those* moments. Open up the 'notes' app on your phone and type in what, exactly, you were doing.

Yes, I know this is dorky. And, yes, I know you're thinking, "I should do that!" And then you're not going to do it.

Do it. I think you'll be surprised by what makes you happy.

3. Remind yourself, "This makes me happy."

Many of the things that make me happy are, to be honest, a hassle (and by 'hassle,' I mean "require me to put on real clothes, google something, and leave the house"). Intellectually, I know taking a day trip to Hudson, working in a new coffee shop, and then hanging out on the sandbar will make me happy ... but it is just SO MUCH EASIER to keep working at home in my yoga pants.

Here's how I remember what makes me happy:

- I wrote a list of the things that make me happy – big and little, easy and difficult – and posted that list next to my computer. Whenever my mind wanders, whenever I'm feeling blue, I can look to the right of my computer screen and remember that reading a chapter of <u>this</u> book while cuddling the dog will make me happy.

- When I'm in the middle of doing something that makes me happy, I say to myself, "This makes me happy."

Am I eating chocolate mousse at a supper club in rural South Dakota? *"This makes me happy."*

Am I hiking around a lake on a sunny Tuesday afternoon? *"This makes me happy."*

I just bought an amazing chair on Craigslist for $50? *"This makes me happy."*

Reciting this little phrase helps cement these happy-making habits in my brain and life. It helps me feel proud to take steps to have the life I want. It reminds me that the hassle of happiness – the planning, the boundary-pushing, the saving, and scheduling – is worth it.

Chapter 20:

10 Habits of Mariah Carey

Mariah Carey has earned not only a "diva" reputation but also a legendary pop icon for over 30 years in the spotlight. She's an American singer-songwriter, actress, and record producer who has lauded her as a "songbird supreme" and the "queen of Christmas." Despite a challenging start, her debut album charted no. 1 in the US, went multi-platinum, and earned her Grammy Awards for Best Female Vocalist and Best Artist. She is one of the most successful female performers of all time, with more than 200 million albums sales landing her a net worth of $320 million. Her distinctive acute euphonies and melismatic runs continues shaping pop music up to date. If you're wondering how this simple New York girl climbed up to becoming this legendary, this is for you! Here are the ten habits of Mariah Carey.

1. Made the Most of What She Was Good At

According to Mariah Carey, she discovered her singing strengths at the age of 6 when her friend, whom she was singing with while holding hands, surprisingly stopped to listen to her. It was from this moment she realized that she had something exceptional and devoted to it. Knowing your strength and devoting entirely to it will eventually land you a lucky spot.

2. Leave No Doubt

Taking your game to the next level can be daunting, and it takes confidence to do so. Mariah Carey's career began magically, but it wasn't long before trolls and haters sprouted. Trolls accused her of being "studio warm" because her voice was so flawless, to be true. She was so troubled by such critics that she decided to shock her detractors with a live performance on MTV.

3. Passion Never Goes Wrong

When Mariah decided to ditch her pop image to focus on R&B and Hip Hop, her decision, as she mentioned in an interview, did not sit well with her record label at first. But eventually resulted to a breakthrough album that is still regarded as the best to date. That's what happens when you believe in your abilities and take a stand for them. Simply put, you're the one who knows how far your abilities can stretch.

4. Forget Plan B, Go Hard on Plan A

To meet your success, you need one well-thought-out plan. With a well-organized plan, make decisions that are in line with your ultimate success objectives. Mariah Carey's music was her life and she was serious and ambitious. Go all in and carry out your only plan as if your life depended on it.

5. Persistence

Perseverance, not talent, is the secret to success. "I knew in my heart that one day I'd make it... Every day that I made it through, I knew I was getting closer to my goal. "Every night, I would thank God for the day when I didn't give up or be knocked down," Carey said in an interview. When you are ambitious, pushing hard is core to achieving your goals.

6. She's All About Equality

If you have a platform, use it to propel influence against societal injustices. Carey received the GLAAD Ally Award in 2016 for her support of the LGBT community. She once assisted one of her backup dancers in proposing to his boyfriend on stage. According to GLAAD CEO Sarah Kate, Mariah Carey has always inspired and encouraged numerous LGBT admirers worldwide with her unwavering commitment to acceptance and inclusive campaigns.

7. A Little Downtime Won't Harm

Mariah mentioned her prior husband's mental and emotional abuse, as well as the chaotic filming of Glitter, in an interview. She worked 22 hours a day, which harmed her mental health and led to her hospitalization in 2001. Your lofty goals demand a healthy mind and body.

8. Explore Constantly

Allow yourself to make mistakes and explore without feeling obligated to deliver a saleable piece every time. Because of Mariah's daring explorations, Male-female collaborative raps and melodies were created by hip hop artists. There's a lot more, but the bottom takeaway is that Maria Carey's daring approach to music paid off.

9. Dream Big

You don't need to know how you'll accomplish the tremendous success you want for yourself; all you need to know is that it will happen. Carey envisioned herself taking off the music industry without doubt and also surpassing Joan Crawford's manor's splendour.

10. Follow Your Superiors

If opportunities don't come knocking at your door, make a door. When Mariah first started recording demos in high school, she met older and more experienced musicians than her. And boy, did she learn! It's also where she worked with Brenda K. Starr, a Puerto Rican freestyle singer. It was through the star that she got noticed by big bosses.

Conclusion

Of course, you don't need to follow suit completely, but you can learn from the divas herself that faith, desire, perseverance, and how serious you take your dreams important manifestation tools.

Chapter 21:

Discomfort Is Temporary

It's easy to get hopeless when things get a little overwhelming. It's easy to give up because you feel you don't have the strength or resources to continue. But where you stop is actually the start you have been looking for since the beginning.

Do you know what you should do when you are broken? You should relish it. You should use it. Because if you know you are broken, congratulations, you have found your limitations.

Now as you know what stopped you last time, you can work towards mending it. You can start to reinforce the breach and you should be able to fill in the cracks in no time.

Life never repeats everything. One day you feel the lowest and the next might bring you the most unpredictable gifts.

The world isn't all sunshine and rainbows. It is a very mean and nasty place to be in. But what can you do now when you are in it? Nothing? Never!

You have to endure the pain, the stress, the discomfort till you are comfortable with the discomfort. It doesn't make any sense, right? But listen to me.

You have a duty towards yourself. You have a duty towards your loved ones. You are expected to rise above all odds and be something no one has ever been before you. I know it might be a little too much to ask for, but, you have to understand your purpose.

Your purpose isn't just to sit on your back and the opportunities and blessings keep coming, knocking at your door, just so you can give up one more time and turn them down.

Things are too easy to reject and neglect but always get hard when you finally step up and go for them. But remember, every breathtaking view is from the top of a hill, but the trek to the top is always tiring. But when you get to the top, you find every cramp worth it.

If you are willing to put yourself through anything, discomfort and temporary small intervals of pain won't affect you in any way. As long as you believe that the experience will bring you to a new level.

If you are interested in the unknown, then you have to break barriers and cross your limits. Because every path that leads to success is full of them. But then and only then you will find yourself in a place where you are unbreakable.

You need to realize that your life is better than most people out there. You need to embrace the pain because all this is temporary. But when you are finally ready to embrace the pain, you are already on your way to a superior being.

Life is all about taking stands because we all get all kinds of blows. But we always need to dig in and keep fighting till we have found the gems or have found our last breath.

The pain and discomfort will subside one day, but if you quit, then you are already on the end of your rope.

Chapter 22:

Happy People Create Time to Do What They Love Every Day

Most of our days are filled with things that we need to do and the things we do to destress ourselves. But, in between all this, we never get time for things. We wanted to do things that bring us pure joy. So then the question is, When will we find time to do what we love? Then, when things calm down a bit and when the people who visit us leave or finish all the trips we have planned and wrap up our busy projects, and the kids will be grown, we will retire? Then, probably after we are dead, we will have more time.

You do not have to wait for things to get less busy or calmer. There will always be something coming up; trips, chores, visitors, errands, holidays, projects, death and illness. There is never going to be more time. Whatever you have been stuck in the past few years, it will always be like that. So now the challenge is not waiting for things to change it is to make time for things you love no matter how busy your life is. Sit down and think about what you want to do, something that you have been putting off. What is something that makes you feel fulfilled and happy? Everyone has those few things that make them fall in love with life think of what is that for you. If you haven't figured it out yet, we will give you some examples, and maybe you can try some of these things and see how that makes you feel.

- Communing with nature

- Going for a beautiful walk

- Creating or growing a business or an organization

- Hiking, running, biking, rowing, climbing

- Meditating, journaling, doing yoga, reflecting

- Communing with loved ones

- Crafting, hogging, blogging, logging, vlogging
- Reading aloud to kids
- Reading aloud to kids

Did you remember something you enjoyed doing, but as the responsibilities kept increasing, you sidelined it. Well, this is your sign to start doing what you loved to take time out for that activity every day, even if it is for 30 minutes only. Carve that time out for yourself, do it now. Once you start doing this, you will realize that you will have more energy because your brain will release serotonin, and your energy level will increase. Secondly, your confidence will improve because you will be making something love every day, and that will constantly help you gain confidence because you will be putting yourself in a happy, self-loving state. You will notice that you have started enjoying life more when you do something you love once a day. It makes the rest of your day brighter and happier. You will also want to constantly continue learning and growing because your brain will strive to do more and more of the thing you like to do, and that will eventually lead to an increased desire of learning and growing. Lastly, your motivation will soar because you will have something to look forward to that brings you pure joy.

Chapter 23:

8 Ways To Gain Self-Confidence

Confidence is not something that can be inherited or learned but is rather a state of mind. Confidence is an attribute that most people would kill to possess. It comes from the feelings of well-being, acceptance of your body and mind (your self-esteem), and belief in your ability, skills, and experience. Positive thinking, knowledge, training, and talking to other people are valuable ways to help improve or boost your confidence levels. Although the definition of self-confidence is different for everyone, the simplest one can be 'to have faith and believe in yourself.'

Here are 8 Ways To Gain More Self-Confidence:

1. Look at what you have already achieved:

It's easy to lose confidence when we dwell on our past mistakes and believe that we haven't actually achieved anything yet. It's common to degrade ourselves and not see our achievements as something special. But we should be proud of ourselves even if we do just a single task throughout the day that benefited us or the society in any way. Please make a list of all the things you are proud of, and it can be as small as cleaning your room or as big as getting a good grade or excelling in your job. Keep adding your small or significant achievements every day. Whenever you feel low in confidence, pull out the list and remind yourself how far you have come, how many amazing things you have done, and how far you still have to go.

2.   Polish the things you're already good at:

We feel confident in the things we know we are good at. Everyone has some kind of strengths, talents, and skills. You just have to recognize what's yours and work towards it to polish it. Some people are naturally good at everything they do. But that doesn't make you any less unique. You have to try to build on those things that you are good at, and they will help you built confidence in your abilities.

3.   Set goals for yourself daily:

Whether it's cooking for yourself, reading a book, studying for a test, planning to meet a friend, or doing anything job-related, make a to-do list for yourself daily. Plan the steps that you have to take to achieve them. They don't necessarily have to be big goals; you should always aim for small achievements. At the end of the day, tick off all the things you did. This will help you gain confidence in your ability to get things done and give you a sense of self-appreciation and self-worth.

4.   Talk yourself up:

That tiny voice inside of our heads is the key player in the game of our lives. You'll always be running low on confidence if that voice constantly has negative commentary in your mind telling you that you're not good enough. You should sit somewhere calm and quiet and talk to yourself out of all the negative things. Treat yourself like you would treat a loved one when they tend to feel down. Convince yourself that you can achieve anything, and there's nothing that can stop you. Fill your mind with positive thoughts and act on them.

5. Get a hobby:

Find yourself something that really interests you. It can either be photography, baking, writing, reading, anything at all. When you have found yourself something you are passionate about, commit yourself to it and give it a go. Chances are, you will get motivated and build skills more quickly; this will help you gain self-confidence as you would gradually get better at it and feel accomplished. The praises you will get for it will also boost your confidence.

6. Face your fears:

The best way to gain confidence is to face your fears head-on. There's no time to apply for a promotion or ask someone out on a date until you feel confident enough. Practice facing your fears even if it means that you will embarrass yourself or mess up. Remind yourself that it's just an experiment. You might learn that making mistakes or being anxious isn't half as bad as you would have thought. It will help you gain confidence each time you move forward, and it will prevent you from taking any risks that will result in negative consequences.

7. Surround yourself with positive people:

Observe your friends and the people around you. Do they lift you and accept who you are or bring you down and point out your flaws? A man is known by the company he keeps. Your friends should always positively influence your thoughts and attitude and make you feel better about yourself.

8. Learn To Strike A Balance:

Self-confidence is not a static measure. Some days, we might feel more confident than others. We might often feel a lack of confidence due to criticism, failures, lack of knowledge, or low self-esteem. While another time we might feel over-confident. We might come off as arrogant and self-centred to other people, and it can eventually lead to our failure. We should keep a suitable amount of confidence within ourselves.

Conclusion:

Confidence is primarily the result of how we have been taught and brought up. We usually learn from others how to behave and what to think of ourselves. Confidence is also a result of our experiences and how we learn to react in different situations. Everyone struggles with confidence issues at one time or another, but these quick fixes should enough to boost your confidence. Start with the easier targets, and then work yourself up. I believe in you. Always!

Chapter 24:

Who Are You Working For?

Who you work for is up to you,

but ultimately every person has a choice in that decision.

Whether you are self-employed, self-made, or salaried,

You determine your own destiny.

As Earl Nightingale said, only the successful will admit it.

You might work for one company your whole life,

but ultimately you are still working for yourself and your family.

If you do not like the practices of your company,

you have the power to leave and make a change.

You must choose to serve who you believe to be worthy of your life.

High self-esteem stops successful people ever feeling subordinate to anyone.

Achieve your goals by envisioning yourself providing quality service in the companies and places that will maximise your chances of success.

Always view yourself as equal to everybody.

All of us have unique talents and qualities within us.

Acknowledg that we can learn from anybody.

Nobody is above or below us.

You can build such qualities that are keys to success.

If one client is taking all your time, reassess his or her value.

If the contract is no longer rewarding, end it as soon as possible.

Doesn't matter if it is a business or personal relationship.

You must get clear on the fact that you are working for you.

You should consider no one your boss.

You should view whoever pays you as a client,

As such you should provide them the best service you can.

Always look to create more opportunity for your business.

Don't look for security - it doesn't exist.

Even if you find it for a time, I guarantee it will be boring at best.

Look for productivity and progression.

Change is definite. It is the only constant.

It will be up to you whether it is progression or regression.

Work with people who have similar goals and objectives.

You should always work with, never for.

Remember that you are always working for yourself.

If working with a company is not bringing you any closer to your goal,

End it now and find one that will.

You should never feel stuck in a job because leaving it is only a letter or phone call away.

You can replace that income in a million different ways.

If you don't like someone scheduling your week for you, start your own business.

If you don't know how, get the training.

Investing in your skills is an investment in your future.

Learning doesn't end with high school.

That was only the beginning – that was practice

Be a life-long learner.

Learn on the job.

Learn so you can achieve more.

Once you admit that you are working for you,

change your bosses title to 'client'.

Open your eyes to a world of other big and wonderful opportunities.

Realize that you are more valuable than you previously believed yourself to be.

Believe you will are incredibly valuable, and you deserve to be paid accordingly.

Whether you are a minimum wage worker or a company director,

you probably haven't even scratched the surface of your capabilities.

Every time someone places limits on what is possible, somebody proves them wrong.

You work for yourself, the possibilities are limitless.

Chapter 25:

How Luck Is Created From Success

Success and luck, just two simple words with meaning more profound than the ocean. These words are interrelated. For everyone, success has a different meaning because everyone has a distant dream to fulfill. Some people want a simple life, but some want to live with the luxuries of life. "Dream big" we all have heard this; setting high goals for the future proves that you believe in yourself, that you can do it after it is only you that can make you a success. Some people believe in luck, but luck goes hand in hand with hard work, determination, creativity. To earn the victory, you will always have to work hard, and you can't just leave everything on luck. But how can you make your luck from success? One may ask.

There are a few simple steps to make your luck. When you face a failure, don't just give up yet, don't ever assume that you can't do anything about the situation. It would be best if you decided to take control. It would help if you believed that you could handle the situation and fix the problems; when has giving up ever been suitable for someone's life. When you decide to take control of things, things turn out to be just fine.

As I said before, believing in yourself is a significant part of making your luck. Do something now. Stop postponing things you want to do, gather some willpower, and do it now before it's too late. Another thing you can do to learn to be lucky is to sit back and make a list of various options; if you can't follow up on one of the options, then go for the other one. Think about as many options as you can; just be creative.

When something holds us back, it is tough for us to move forward, or when you are stuck at the same routine and are not doing anything to move forward, luck can do nothing about your laziness. Take out time for yourself and decide about how you will move forward, how you will grow. Consider every single alternative out there. After determining what you want to do in the future, seek the opportunities. Whenever you think you have a chance, take action; now is not the time to sit back and watch; it is the time to run and grab that opportunity because you never know when the next time will come.

Successful people are committed to the fact that they want to be in control of their lives; that is how you make your luck from your success. It's all about believing in yourself.

Chapter 26:

Happy People Are Busy but Not Rushed

Dan Pink points to an interesting new research finding — the happiest people are those that are very busy but don't feel rushed:

Who among us are the happiest? Newly published research suggests that fortunate folks have little or no excess time and yet seldom feel rushed.

This clicks with me. I love blogging, but I hate being under time pressure to get it done. This tension is very nicely demonstrated in a recent study by Hsee et al. (2010). When given a choice, participants preferred to do nothing unless given the tiniest possible reason to do something: a piece of candy. Then they sprang into action.

Not only did people only need the smallest inducement to keep busy, but they were also happier when doing something rather than nothing. It's as if people understand that being busy will keep them happier, but they need an excuse of some kind.

Having plenty of time gives you a feeling of control. Anything that increases your *perception of control* over a situation (whether it increases your control or not) can substantially decrease your stress level.

In Colorado, Steve Maier at the University of Boulder says that the degree of control that organisms can exert over something that creates stress determines whether the stressor alters the organism's functioning. His findings indicate that only uncontrollable stressors cause harmful effects. Inescapable or uncontrollable stress can be destructive, whereas the same stress that feels escapable is less destructive, significantly so... **Over and over, scientists see that the perception of control over a stressor alters the stressor's impact.**

But heavy time pressure stresses you out and kills creativity. Low-to-moderate time pressure produces the best results.

If managers regularly set impossibly short time-frames or impossibly high workloads, employees become stressed, unhappy, and unmotivated—burned out. Yet, people hate being bored. It was rare for any participant in our study to report a day with very low time pressure, such days—when they did occur—were also not conducive to positive inner work life. In general, low-to-moderate time pressure seems optimal for sustaining positive thoughts, feelings, and drives.

Your reaction to being too busy and under time pressure might be to want to do nothing. But that can drop you into the bottom left corner. And this makes you more unhappy than anything:

...**surveys "continue to show the least happy group to be those who quite often have excess time." Boredom, it seems, is burdensome.**

So, stay busy—set goals. Challenge yourself, but make sure you have plenty of time to feel in control of the situation.

This is how games feel. And games are fun.

Chapter 27:
Ten Habits Of The Rich And
Successful

The rich and successful have common habits. Some of them have walked down the same path to glory.

Wealth is not measured in terms of properties only but also the strength of character. One can be rich in wisdom but not as much in properties. Nevertheless, they are considered rich and successful because they have an abundance of an intangible asset – wisdom.

Here are ten habits of the rich and successful:

1. <u>They Are Generous</u>

Rich and successful people are often generous because they know what it feels like to lack. Even those born in rich families are generous because they probably have seen their parents helping the needy.

Most rich people globally have foundations in their name. It is not a channel to wealth for themselves, but a means to do acts of charity. The Bill & Melinda gates foundation, for example, has helped the most vulnerable globally during a famine, war, and even during the coronavirus disease pandemic.

2. <u>They Read Widely</u>

Successful people read a lot. The reading culture in them developed at an early age and could have most likely molded them into the people they are. Great leaders are readers. As leaders of giant corporates, it is important to be well vast with the wisdom of other great people.

Reading is not capped at any age. Successful people know that learning is continuous and apply the knowledge from the literature they read in their lives. Reading lightens the burden of management on the shoulders of the rich who are directors in their companies.

3. They Are Not Workaholics

It is amazing how one can be wealthy and successful without being a workaholic. Ironically, most workaholics are not as rich as you would expect. Despite them foregoing a lot of things for the sake of their work, they cannot match the rich who work only a few hours a day.

It is not the amount of time you work but the quality of work you do. Work holism will rob you of your social life and you will be depressed. Apportion equal time in everything you do, not only your work.

4. They Are Social People

One would think that most rich and successful people are arrogant or anti-social. This is untrue. They are social and outgoing. You will find them in their social circles over coffee or playing golf. They are approachable and receptive to new ideas.

Reaching them is indeed difficult because of their security or protocol to follow before talking to them. They have security because of their high profile and they could be targets of bad people. Nevertheless, they are very engaging when you get to know them.

5. They Have Trust Issues

Most rich people are insecure because of their wealth. They rarely trust strangers because their intentions are unknown. Some of them have been shortchanged in their business dealings and cannot easily trust again.

When interacting with them, do not take offense to their mistrust. Instead, try to win their trust slowly until they realize that you are genuine. It is only then that they will trust you with their work or build a friendship with you.

6. <u>They Are Never Idle</u>

An idle mind is the devil's workshop. The rich and successful know this too well. You may be tempted into doing immoral acts when you have a lot of idle time at your disposal. Engage yourself willfully in productive activities lest you are lured into vices because you have a lot of free time. This is not a call to work holism. It is okay to have free time to spend out of your busy schedule, but that time should be planned for carefully. Like the rich and successful, your mind should always be occupied with positive thoughts and plans on how you can progress.

7. <u>They Have A Flexible Mindset</u>

The rich and successful do not lead rigid lives. They have a flexible mindset that makes them open to other business ideas and suggestions. Their ears listen to consumer needs in the market and they develop products and services to meet those needs.

It is often misconceived that successful people live in their zone and are indifferent to common people. The truth is that they became successful by being open-minded. A fixed mind is an enemy of progress.

8. <u>They Are Bold</u>

Wealthy people are bold and make public statements without any fear of backlash. Boldness is a sign of being an alpha.

As much as their wealth could be insulation against any repercussions, people pay attention when the rich give their opinions because they are unsure of their motive. When a successful person boldly gives their opinion, it is taken seriously because it has the potential to influence market forces.

9. They Consult Widely

The rich are not always wise; even the wise seek counsel. Before they make any significant action, they seek advice from people they trust. They then weigh the pros and cons of what they intended to do and make an informed choice.

Unlike common people who act out of impulse, the rich take advice from trusted sources (mostly professionals) very seriously. Rarely do they err, always hitting the nail on the head. You should consider consulting before acting if you want to be like the rich.

10. They Are Visionary

Vision is often misconstrued for sight. It is getting the bigger picture without losing grip on fine details. Were it not for the eagle vision of the successful, they could not be able to maintain their status. Rich people know the direction they are going and they work towards it.

Vision is not an innate trait; it is developed over time. You will need to be visionary and not get distracted as you chart your way towards richness. Take this cue from successful people.

In conclusion, we acknowledge that the rich and successful run the world. When you start practicing their habits, you will soon be like them.

Chapter 28:

Happy People Celebrate Other People's Success

What a phony smile… Why do people want him? How has he accomplished anything? It's ME they need. I'm the one who should be successful, not him. What a joke." This was my inner dialogue when I heard about other people's success. Like a prima donna, I seethed with jealousy and couldn't stand to hear about people doing better than me.

But all the hating got me nowhere. So I thought about who I was really mad at…it wasn't the successful people I raged at. When I got more serious about succeeding, I channeled that useless envy into accepting myself.

I practiced self-acceptance with a journal, through affirmations, and by encouraging myself—especially when I failed. Then something weird happened. I started feeling happy for other people's success. Without a hint of irony, I congratulated people on their hard work, and I applauded their success with my best wishes. It felt good. I felt more successful doing it.

> **"Embrace your uniqueness. Time is much too short to be living someone else's life." – Kobi Yamada**

My writing career caught fire at the same time. I was published on sites that I'd only dreamt of, and whose authors I had cussed for doing things that the egotistical me still hadn't. Congratulating others started a positive feedback loop. The more I accepted myself, the more I celebrated other people's success and the more I celebrated their success, the more success I achieved. Now that I look back, I could've hacked my growth curve by celebrating others' success as a daily ritual.

1. It conditions you for your own success

Feeling good for someone else's success helps you generate the same feelings you need for your own accomplishments. So put yourself in the other's shoes. Revel in their accomplishments; think of all the hard work that went into it. Celebrate their success and know that soon you'll experience the same thing for yourself. Apply the good feelings to your visions for a brighter future.

2. You'll transcend yourself

Everyone knows that to actually succeed, you need to be part of something bigger. But most people are kept from that bigger something by wanting all the focus for themselves. it's an ego issue.

Through celebrating others, you'll practice the selflessness it takes to let go of your tiny shell and leap into the ocean of success that comes through serving others. Cheer your fellow entrepreneurs. Feel their success. Let go of your want for recognition and accept that you'll get it when you help enough other people.

Chapter 29:

5 Tips to Increase Your Attention Span

If you've ever found it difficult to get through a challenging task at work, studied for an important exam, or spent time on a finicky project, you might have wished you could increase your ability to concentrate.

Concentration refers to the mental effort you direct toward whatever you're working on or learning at the moment. It's sometimes confused with attention span, but attention span refers to the length of time you can concentrate on something.

If that sounds familiar, keep reading to learn more about research-backed methods to help improve your attention span. We'll also go over some conditions that can affect concentration and steps to take if trying to increase concentration on your own just doesn't seem to help.

1. Train Your Brain
Playing certain types of games can help you get better at concentrating. Try:

- sudoku

- crossword puzzles

- chess

- jigsaw puzzles

- word searches or scrambles

- memory games

Results of a 2015 study Trusted Source of 4,715 adults suggest spending 15 minutes a day, five days a week, on brain training activities can greatly impact concentration.

Brain training games can also help you develop your working and short-term memory, as well as your processing and problem-solving skills.

Older adults

The effects of brain training games may be particularly important for older adults since memory and concentration often tend to decline with age.

Research from 2014Trusted Source that looked at 2,832 older adults followed up on participants after ten years. Older adults who completed between 10 and 14 cognitive training sessions saw improved cognition, memory, and processing skills.

After ten years, most study participants reported they could complete daily activities at least as well as they could at the beginning of the trial, if not better.

2. Get Your Game On

Brain games may not be the only type of game that can help improve concentration. Newer research also suggests playing video games could help boost concentration.

A 2018 study looking at 29 people found evidence to suggest an hour of gaming could help improve visual selective attention (VSA). VSA refers to your ability to concentrate on a specific task while ignoring distractions around you.

Its small size limited this study, so these findings aren't conclusive. The study also didn't determine how long this increase in VSA lasted.

Study authors recommend future research continue exploring how video games can help increase brain activity and boost concentration.

3. Improve Sleep

Sleep deprivation can easily disrupt concentration, not to mention other cognitive functions, such as memory and attention.

Occasional sleep deprivation may not cause too many problems for you. But regularly failing to get a good night's sleep can affect your mood and performance at work.

Being too tired can even slow down your reflexes and affect your ability to drive or do other daily tasks.

A demanding schedule, health issues, and other factors sometimes make it difficult to get enough sleep. But it's important to try and get as close to the recommended amount as possible on most nights.

Many experts recommend adults aim for 7 to 8 hours of sleep each night.

4. Make Time For Exercise

Increased concentration is among the many benefits of regular exercise. Exercise benefits everyone. A 2018 study looking at 116 fifth-graders found evidence to suggest daily physical activity could help improve both concentration and attention after just four weeks.

Another Source looking at older adults suggests that just a year of moderate aerobic physical activity can help stop or reverse memory loss that occurs with brain atrophy related to age.

Do what you can

Although aerobic exercise is recommended, doing what you can is better than doing nothing at all. Depending on your fitness and weight goals, you may want to exercise more or less.

But sometimes, it just isn't possible to get the recommended amount of exercise, especially if you live with physical or mental health challenges.

5. Spend Time In Nature

If you want to boost your concentration naturally, try to get outside every day, even for just 15 to 20 minutes. You might take a short walk through a park. Sitting in your garden or backyard can also help. Any natural environment has benefits.

Scientific evidence increasingly supports the positive impact of natural environments. Research from 2014Trusted Source found evidence to suggest including plants in office spaces helped increase concentration and productivity and workplace satisfaction, and air quality.

Try adding a plant or two to your workspace or home for a range of positive benefits. Succulents make great choices for low-maintenance plants if you don't have a green thumb.

Chapter 30:

Ten Ways To Build New Habits by Taking Advantage of Old Ones

You may have heard that old habits die hard or that a leopard never changes its spots. It is easier to build new habits on old ones than to form them from scratch.

These are ten ways to build new habits by taking advantage of old ones:'

1. Replacing Strategy

This is a psychological strategy of deceiving the mind that you are following your old habits while it is not the case. It works best if you had an addiction that you want to get rid of. For example, alcoholics who want to reform can replace beer with soft drinks or even coffee and take it at the same time they use to take a beer.

The new habit will gradually overshadow the old one and after some time it will be completely gone.

2. Change Your Company

Take an audit of your friends and their habits and you will observe that you share some things, including the habit you want to get rid of. You cannot overcome it if you are constantly in their company because of the influence they have over you.

Take a step of distancing yourself from them and watch yourself adapting to the new habits you desire. In their absence, you will find other friends with whom you will share the new lifestyle of your choice.

3. Engage In Sports and Recreational Activities

So powerful is sports that it unites warring sides and rival communities. Spend the time you used to do a habit you want to abandon to engage in any kind of sports. It is a good replacement for that time and it exposes you to other people who may influence you to other new positive habits. Moreover, you will be exhausted after the games and will not have the time to return to your old habit.

4. Invest Your Time in Researching On Demerits of Your Old Habits

Divert your energy, time, and resources to researching the harm they cause instead of engaging in them. You will be enlightened and with the knowledge build a new habit of creating awareness about the same to save other people.

You will effectively create a new habit to replace the undesirable older one.

5. Use The Old Habit As A Motivation For A New One

When life gives you lemons, make lemonade. Leverage the positive aspect of every situation including your old habits to create new ones. The motivation to abandon your old ways will help you build new habits that are the opposite of the old ones.

This is effective especially if you want to build a reputable reputation.

6. Combine Two Habits

You can combine two habits to help build a new one if you want to retain all of them. You can clean the house while singing and dancing to your favorite song. You will ride on the singing and dancing to fortify your cleaning skills.

This method will make you an all-around person and likable.

7. Express An Old Habit In A New Way

New habits are not always new. They can be a recreation of old habits.

Change how you approach issues to give birth to a new habit.

If you love storytelling, for example, consider doing the same through

blogs or videos. In the process, you will adopt a writing habit.

8. Seek Professional Guidance

If you are comfortable sharing your experiences with somebody else, talk

to a professional counselor or a trustworthy person. They will be your

light and advice you on the path to pursue when you are in limbo.

When we have fully discovered ourselves, we can build new habits on old

ones. At times, we need the guidance of experienced people and

professionals to discover our hidden abilities.

9. Change of Environment

Our environments play a significant role in unearthing our potential.

Different environments have different challenges to which we adjust differently. Sometimes a change in our environments is important to help us develop new habits from our old ones.

We could be blind to how we can use our old habits to our advantage when we are in one place for a long time.

10. Seek Financial Freedom

Building new habits from old ones could sometimes require some funding. For example, you may want to go to the movies but you are unable to finance that. When you are financially stable, you can easily adjust yourself in situations that require financial muscles.

In conclusion, these ten habits are not the only ones to help build new habits by leveraging on old ones. They are however the most effective ones.

Chapter 31:

<u>Stop Ignoring Your Health</u>

Do you have a busy life? Do you follow a hard and continuous regime of tasks every day for a significant amount of time? Have you ever felt that you cannot enjoy even the happiest moments of your life even if you want to? Let me highlight one reason you might recognize it straight away.

You are not enjoying your days while still being in all your senses because you don't have your mind and body in the right place.

All these years you have lived your life as a race. You have taken part in every event in and around your life just because you never wanted to miss anything. But in this process, you never lived your life to its full potential. You never lived a single moment with just the emotional intention of being then and there and not trying to live it like just another day or event.

People often get so busy with making their careers that they don't realize what is more important in life? It is their mental and physical health!

You will not get anywhere far in your life if you keep ignoring the signs of sickness your body keeps giving you. Your body is a machine with a conditional warranty. The day you violate the conditions of this warranty, life will become challenging and you won't even be interested in the basic tasks at hand.

You might have heard the famous saying that "Health is Wealth". Let it sink in for a while and analyze your own life. You don't need to be a top-tier athlete to have a good body. You need a good body for your organs to work properly. You need an active lifestyle to be more productive and be more present and engaged in the things that are going around you.

The dilemma of our lives is that we don't care about what we have right now, but we care a lot about what we want. Not realizing that what we want might be cursed but what we have is the soul of good living. And that my friends are the blessing of health that most of us take for granted.

Most people have a tendency and devotion to work specifically on their health and fitness on a priority basis. They have a better standard of life. These people have a clearer mind to feel and capture the best moments in life with what their senses can offer best to them.

If you don't stop ignoring your health, you won't ever get out of this constant struggle. The struggle to find the reasons for you being detached from everything despite being involved every time.

Being careful and observant of your health doesn't make you selfish. This makes you a much more caring person because not only your life but the life of others around you is also affected by your sickness. Not only your resources are used for your treatments but the attention and emotions of your loved ones are also being spent, just in hope of your wellness.

Chapter 32:

Happy People Spend Time Alone

No man is an island except for similarly as we blossom with human contact and connections, so too would we be able to prosper from time burned through alone. Also, this, maybe, turns out to be particularly important right now since we're all in detachment. We've since quite a while ago slandered the individuals who decide to be distant from everyone else, except isolation shouldn't be mistaken for forlornness. Here are two mental reasons why investing energy in isolation makes us more joyful and more satisfied:

1. Spending time alone reconnects us.

Our inclination for isolation might be transformative, as indicated by an examination distributed in the British Journal of Psychology in 2016. Utilizing what they call "the Savannah hypothesis of satisfaction," transformative clinicians Satoshi Kanazawa of the London School of Economics and Norman Li of Singapore Management University accept that the single, tracker accumulate way of life of our precursors structure the establishment of what satisfies us in present-day times. The group examined a study of 15,000 individuals matured somewhere between 18 and 28 in the United States. They found that individuals living in more thickly populated regions were fundamentally less cheerful than the individuals who lived in more modest networks.

"The higher the populace thickness of the prompt climate, the less glad" respondents were. The scientists accept this is because we had advanced mentally from when mankind, for the most part, existed on distant, open savannahs. Since quite a while ago, we have instilled an inclination to be content alone, albeit current life generally neutralizes that. Also, as good to beat all, they tracked down that the more clever an individual was, the more they appreciated investing energy alone. Along these lines, isolation makes you more joyful AND is evidence of your smarts. We're in.

2. Spending Time Alone Teaches Us Empathy

Investing in a specific measure of energy alone can create more compassion towards others than a milestone concentrate from Harvard. Scientists found that when enormous gatherings of individuals encircle us, it's harder for us to acquire viewpoints and tune into the sensations of others. However, when we venture outside that unique circumstance, the extra headspace implies we can feel for the situation of individuals around us in a more genuine and significant manner. Furthermore, that is uplifting news for others, but different investigations show that compassion and helping other people are significant to prosperity and individual satisfaction.

"At the point when you invest energy with a specific friend network or your colleagues, you foster a 'we versus them' attitude," clarifies psychotherapist and creator Amy Morin. "Investing energy alone assists you with growing more empathy for individuals who may not find a way into your 'inward circle.' "On the off chance that you're not used to isolation, it can feel awkward from the outset," she adds. "However, making that tranquil time for yourself could be critical to turning into the best form of yourself."

Chapter 33:

8 Ways To Love Yourself First

"Your task is not to seek for love, but merely to seek and find all the barriers within yourself that you have built against it." - Rumi.

Most of us are so busy waiting for someone to come into our lives and love us that we have forgotten about the one person we need to love the most – ourselves. Most psychologists agree that being loved and being able to love is crucial to our happiness. As quoted by Sigmund Freud, "love and work ... work and love. That's all there is." It is the mere relationship of us with ourselves that sets the foundation for all other relationships and reveals if we will have a healthy relationship or a toxic one.

Here are some tips on loving yourself first before searching for any kind of love in your life.

1. Know That Self-Love Is Beautiful

Don't ever consider self-love as being narcissistic or selfish, and these are two completely different things. Self-love is rather having positive regard for our wellbeing and happiness. When we adopt self-love, we see higher levels of self-esteem within ourselves, are less critical and harsh with ourselves while making mistakes, and can celebrate our positive qualities and accept all our negative ones.

2. Always be kind to yourself:

We are humans, and humans are tended to get subjected to hurts, shortcomings, and emotional pain. Even if our family, friends, or even our partners may berate us about our inadequacies, we must learn to accept ourselves with all our imperfections and flaws. We look for acceptance from others and be harsh on ourselves if they tend to be cruel or heartless with us. We should always focus on our many positive qualities, strengths, and abilities, and admirable traits; rather than harsh judgments, comparisons, and self-hatred get to us. Always be gentle with yourself.

3. Be the love you feel within yourself:

You may experience both self-love and self-hatred over time. But it would be best if you always tried to focus on self-love more. Try loving yourself and having positive affirmations. Do a love-kindness meditation or spiritual practices to nourish your soul, and it will help you feel love and compassion toward yourself. Try to be in that place of love throughout your day and infuse this love with whatever interaction you have with others.

4. Give yourself a break:

We don't constantly live in a good phase. No one is perfect, including ourselves. It's okay to not be at the top of your game every day, or be happy all the time, or love yourself always, or live without pain. Excuse your bad days and embrace all your imperfections and mistakes. Accept your negative emotions but don't let them overwhelm you. Don't set high standards for yourself, both emotionally and mentally. Don't judge yourself for whatever you feel, and always embrace your emotions wholeheartedly.

5. Embrace yourself:

Are you content to sit all alone because the feelings of anxiety, fear, guilt, or judgment will overwhelm you? Then you have to practice being comfortable in your skin. Go within and seek solace in yourself, practice moments of alone time and observe how you treat yourself. Allow yourself to be mindful of your beliefs, feelings, and thoughts, and embrace solitude. The process of loving yourself starts with understanding your true nature.

6. Be grateful:

Rhonda Bryne, the author of The Magic, advises, "When you are grateful for the things you have, no matter how small they may be, you will see those things instantly increase." Look around you and see all the things that you are blessed to have. Practice gratitude daily and be thankful for all the things, no matter how good or bad they are. You will immediately start loving yourself once you realize how much you have to be grateful for.

7. Be helpful to those around you:

You open the door for divine love the moment you decide to be kind and compassionate toward others. "I slept and dreamt that life was a joy. I awoke and saw that life was service. I acted, and behold, and service was a joy." - Rabindranath Tagore. The love and positive vibes that you wish upon others and send out to others will always find a way back to you. Your soul tends to rejoice when you are kind, considerate, and compassionate. You have achieved the highest form of self-love when you decide to serve others. By helping others, you will realize that you don't need someone else to feel complete; you are complete. It will help you feel more love and fulfillment in your life.

8. Do things you enjoy doing:

If you find yourself stuck in a monotonous loop, try to get some time out for yourself and do the things that you love. There must be a lot of hobbies and passions that you might have put a brake on. Dust them off and start doing them again. Whether it's playing any sport, learning a new skill, reading a new book, writing in on your journal, or simply cooking or baking for yourself, start doing it again. We shouldn't compromise on the things that make us feel alive. Doing the things we enjoy always makes us feel better about ourselves and boost our confidence.

Conclusion:

Loving yourself is nothing short of a challenge. It is crucial for your emotional health and ability to reach your best potential. But the good news is, we all have it within us to believe in ourselves and live the best life we possibly can. Find what you are passionate about, appreciate yourself, and be grateful for what's in your life. Accept yourself as it is.

Chapter 34:

7 Ways To Develop Effective Communication With Your Clients

Effective communication is a significant factor in business; it is the essence of your business as clients are the core of every business. Sometimes, we forget what the client wanted; if this has happened to you, then you that your communication skills need a tad bit of improvement. The relationships you build with your clients are the key. Gaining loyal customers is essential, as they buy from you repeatedly and refer you to others, which increases customers. Communication can take many shapes and forms; it can be formal or informal and can happen over various platforms. Here are seven ways to develop practical communication skills with your clients.

1. Make It About Your Clients

When you meet someone that requires your services, you need to make it about them. It would help if you indeed gained your client's trust, but that doesn't mean the client has to hear your whole life story or several awards you have won. So whenever a new client seeks out help, remember that it is them that need help and focus on how you can impress them and meet their requirements. It is the best way to demonstrate your experience and extensive knowledge about the subject.

2. Treat Them How You'd Like To Be Treated

Business can be very tiring, sometimes when the stress is overbearing, we might feel moody and irritated but try not to take out the irritation on the clients, as your business exists because of your clients, so being rude with them will not be very wise. Try to be more patient, friendly, and positive with them, and your positive behavior shows your eagerness for your work. So try to treat your customers the most excellent way possible, the way you would want to be treated.

3. Respect Your Client's Time

"Time is money" we all have heard this famous saying, but what does it mean? The sentence gives away its meaning. It means that time is precious, whether it's yours or your clients'. Hence, try to avoid talking too much or wasting their time. Try not to make them wait for you too much that may cause unhealthiness in your relationship with your client. Try to get to the point without sounding rude or being blunt, be concise. Over media platforms, a short and well-planned consultation probably will do the work, and if they need any more information, they would ask you.

4. Listen To Your Clients

We all have met that annoying salesman that doesn't understand what you want or doesn't let you finish. If you have met someone like that, you know how irritating it could be, so when it is your time to be a businessman, don't do the same. When talking to your clients, please give them your undivided attention; you could do that by clearing up your brain of everything, no matter how busy the day is and how long the to-do list is. Take notes if you think you need them; try not to interrupt and stay silent if you think the customer wants to add a few more points. Listen actively to the client so that you can provide better customer service.

5. Pay Attention To What Your Clients Say

Any relationship requires attention; without attention, a client may seem very happy, and your business might not flourish the way you want it to. So pay attention to the tiniest of details of what the clients say. Take notes of the information that is hard to remember or seems essential. Ensure that you respond to emails, requests, or questions about your business; it will make the clients feel important. When sending out an email to your clients, double-check and see if you had made any mistakes, grammar mistakes indicate carelessness, and what kind of a client would want a careless person to help them.

6. **Actively Build Your Client Communication Skills**

If you want to create a lasting relationship with your customers, focus on your communication skills; you could set up a few rules and principles for yourself and your team to follow—brief your team on how to be friendly and provide the customer service required by the client. You can ask your client for their feedback on customer service; if they share something they don't like, you and your team can together work on that. Also, use client communication tools and software.

7. **Keep Records of Your Interactions**

Always keep records of your previous conversations with your clients; if you forgot a minor detail that was not so minor for them, it might not end pleasantly. Even the people who give clients their undivided attention forget things. So you could keep records of your interactions with your clients by making notes on a file or your mobile phone or by recording the conversation after they allow you. Making notes will also help you later, as it will help you remember who you need to check up on or follow up with.

Conclusion

Try to follow these ways, and win the trust of your clients. Be friendly and pleasant, and your clients will stay happy with you.

Chapter 35:
10 Reasons Money Can't Buy You Happiness

I'm sure you have heard this statement before, that "Money can't buy happiness.", but have you stopped to think about why it might be so? Many of us chase money and that high paying job because we believe that it will bring us wealth which will in turn make us happy. We do it because it is what society tells us we should be doing. That we should trade all our time and energy to make money no matter how many sacrifices we have to make with regards to our friendships, relationships, and so on.

It is true that a certain income level and money in the bank is required to allow us to have a comfortable standard of living, which could make life quite nice for us. But beyond that, it will be tough to derive happiness from just sheer truckloads of money alone, as we will soon find out.

1. Our Happiness Is Not Derived From Material Things

This is arguably the most important yet easily overlooked aspect when it comes to dealing with money. While most of us will have desires to live in a dream home, owning the ultimate luxury car, and buying the greatest gifts we can buy when we're rich, we fail to realize that the process of acquisition of material things is a futile effort. It is always thrilling to be on the forefront of owning the latest material good on the market, but the excitement you have for a product usually fades away pretty quickly once you have them in your hands. We acclimatize very quickly to what we have, and we search for the next thing almost immediately. This seemingly endless chase for happiness would seem like a carrot on a stick, always dangling it's juiciness in front of you but you never get to taste it. If you look around at the things you have in your house, you will know what I mean. All the stuff that was once intriguing to you now no longer has the same effect of joy and happiness that it once had. Bottom line is that there is no amount of stuff you can acquire that will ever make you truly happy.

2. Money Cannot Buy You Relationships

We fail to realize the power of relationships when it comes to the happiness equation. Happiness can easily be derived from thriving relationships. Relationships that serve to enrich our lives in all aspects of it. When we are in a relationship with someone who loves and cares for us unconditionally, there is no amount of money that can buy you that feeling. The same goes for friendships and family. Having people that support you in your endeavors, grieve with you when you experience loss, or just someone you can talk to, to share your feelings of excitement, sorrow, and all the different ranges of emotions, those are the moments that truly matter in life.

3. Money Could Lure Disingenuous People

While some may argue that you can buy friendships by paying people to be around you, I am pretty sure most of you wouldn't want to go down that path. You know that these people are not hanging around you because they like you, but because they like what you have in your pocket. Genuine relationships are ones that will last even when you don't have a dime left in your back account. When all else fails, you will want to have these people around you for support.

4. You Will Never Feel Like You have Enough Money

Chasing money as a substitute for happiness is a tricky thing. We all think we need $1 million dollars in our bank account to be happy, but as soon as we hit that milestone, something just doesn't feel quite right. We feel empty inside, we feel like maybe it's not enough, so we set a bigger target of $2 million. But that day will come too and again we will feel like something is amiss. The cycle repeats itself until we finally realize that deriving happiness from a monetary goal is also a futile effort.

5. Money Only Helps To Improve Your Standard of Living

Instead of using money as bait for happiness, use it for what it really is for - survival, food, clothing, a roof over your head, and the occasional splurge on something you like. Beyond that, look elsewhere for happiness. I am here to tell you that it is human nature for us to feel like we never have enough of something, and that includes money. We have been programmed to always want and need more. More of everything. We compare to people more successful than us and think we need to live like them in order to be happy. Don't make the same mistake as everyone else. Find a comfortable amount you need for survival and retirement, and the rest is bonus.

6. Making Money Requires Sacrifices

Unless you're a trust fund baby, or money falls from the sky, or you managed to strike a jackpot, constantly putting money above all else requires time and effort to earn. Working 12 hour shifts, 7 days a week is no easy feat. You will see your youth fly by and your other priorities fall by the wayside. By the time you've earned the desired income of your dreams, you may well find that a few decades have passed and you're standing on top of the mountain, alone, with no one to share that experience with. No one who may be able to travel with you or even spend that money with you. Unless you consciously try for a balanced work-life, you will find it quite a lonesome experience.

7. The Simple Pleasures In Life Doesn't Require That Much Money

Spending time with your family, going out for coffee with friends, having a chill board games night on the weekends with enthusiasts like yourself, you will find that all these activities brings us closer to the emotional world. The emotional and spiritual connection we have with fellow human beings that bring us laughter, joy, sadness, and happiness. We fail to realize that the happiest moments we can create doesn't require that much money. It just requires planning and some food. Stop chasing the dream vacation halfway around the world for happiness. It is underneath you all along.

8. You Lack the Happiness Mindset

Happiness is merely a feeling, and feelings can be created by choice. Money can't fix your emotional problems, it can only buy you therapy. Ultimately, it's your attitude and mindset that determines your level of happiness that you experience. If you always see the glass half empty, no amount of money can make you see the glass as half full.

9. You Don't Feel Grateful for The Things Money Buy You

We take for granted the things we have acquired so far and only look towards the next shiny object. Being grateful for our hard-earned money has bought us thus far should be our number one priority. Treasure the bed you bought that you can sleep comfortably in, be thankful for the television you have that allows you to stream your favourite shows on demand, be grateful for the roof that houses all these items and protects you from the elements.

10. We Fall into The If-Then Trap of Chasing Money

How many times do you have the thought that the next promotion you receive will be the happiest moment of your life. Or perhaps that your boss will give me a raise if you turn this project in successfully. If we only chase our paychecks rather than chase fulfillment, we are running the wrong race in life.

Remember these important points the next time you work for money. Yes, having money is important, but it should not adversely affect your ability to live a fulfilling life. There are a million other things that are just as equally important if you're chasing happiness.

CPSIA information can be obtained
at www.ICGtesting.com
Printed in the USA
LVHW050018140122
708530LV00014B/531